The Gospel of the Kingdom

The Gospel of the Kingdom

Lance Lambert

LANCE LAMBERT MINISTRIES

Richmond, VA

ISBN 978-1-68389-073-7
www.lancelambert.org

Contents

Preface

The following messages on *The Gospel of The Kingdom* were presented by Lance Lambert at the Christian Family Conference held in Richmond, VA during June 1990. His spoken words have been transcribed into this book and edited only for clarity.

And this gospel of the kingdom shall be preached in
the whole world for a testimony unto all the nations;
and then shall the end come. (Matthew 24:14)

The following words from Lance Lambert sum up the burden that the Lord discharged during that time:

This gospel of the kingdom of God; this gospel concerning God's King; this gospel concerning the abounding grace of God by which He gives us the possibility of coming to the throne of God, by the grace of God alone; this gospel of the glory of God; this gospel of our Lord Jesus; this gospel has been entrusted to those who are followers of the Lord Jesus to be preached in the whole world. We have no business to be disengaged from this commission. I want to put it in the strongest language possible. It is a sin and a transgression for the people of God not to be involved practically, relevantly in the preaching of this gospel of the kingdom in the whole world.

May the Lord's people respond to this commission.

1.
Kingship

Matthew 4:23

And Jesus went about in all Galilee, teaching in their synagogues, and preaching the gospel of the kingdom, and healing all manner of disease and all manner of sickness among the people.

Matthew 9:35

And Jesus went about all the cities and the villages, teaching in their synagogues, and preaching the gospel of the kingdom, and healing all manner of disease and all manner of sickness.

Matthew 24:14

And this gospel of the kingdom shall be preached in the whole world for a testimony unto all the nations; and then shall the end come.

Shall we pray:

Lord, we are so thankful that we are able to meet in this simple way in Your presence. We thank You that we are gathering together not supremely to a place nor supremely to a people but we are gathering together to Yourself. And Lord, as we are found here in Your presence, we want to ask that You will graciously endow us with the Holy Spirit both in the speaking and in the hearing. We need You, Lord. I can outline truths, we can hear truths, we can learn much academically; but what we need in these days is to meet with You. We need Your Word to come and dwell in us richly in all wisdom. We need that implanted Word, that Word which will take root in us and will grow up and bear much fruit. To that end, Lord, we thank You that You have provided us with all that we need for this conference and for this our opening time together. By faith we stand into that anointing both for my speaking and for our hearing, that You will wonderfully, deeply, fully meet all our needs. Be manifested in our weakness my weakness in speaking and our weakness in hearing that, Lord, it may be Your Word that is spoken and Your Word that is heard and received. We give ourselves afresh to You in the name of our Lord Jesus. Amen.

There are many errors that, at present, are being propagated over the kingdom of God, many things that bring grief and pain to those of us who love the Lord and who long, above everything else, that His kingdom shall come. Above all people, those of us who are born of God should have an experience of the kingdom of God.

For us, the kingdom of God has arrived. It has come in our hearts; it has brought us into a union with God through the

Messiah, Jesus. It has brought us into a marvelous experience of eternal life, an ever deepening discovery of those unsearchable riches of the Lord Jesus, that fathomless fulness of God. But, of course, there is a kingdom that is going to come outwardly. First and foremost, it must come inwardly to us as individuals and as the church of God. We must know in our experience the rule of God. We must know the reign of the Lord Jesus. We must be truly and genuinely led by the Spirit of God.

However, there is coming a day when the kingdom of God will come literally and when the kingdom of this world will become the kingdom of God and of His Messiah forever. I don't know how far away that day is, but I suspect that we are very near to it. All the signs on every side seem to point to the coming, finally, of the kingdom of God. It is a literal kingdom that is coming; it is a literal King that is coming. It is the very same Jesus who walked this earth for thirty-three years whose feet are again going to stand upon this earth. Very sadly, many Christians, because they want to be truly spiritual and to know the Lord spiritually, have almost made the Lord Jesus the Spirit of God, as if He is (may I put it reverently) faceless, as if He has no human form, as if He will never again walk as a human being. But the Lord Jesus is the Son of Man forever. He is God's Messiah and, one day, He is coming back literally. You will actually see Him. He will be a human being even with marks in His hands and in His side and in His feet. It is the same Jesus. It is wonderful to consider this because, if the Lord Jesus is literally coming back as the Son of Man, as the Messiah, as King of kings and Lord of lords, as King of the Jews, King of Israel, as Head of the church, then the kingdom that is coming with Him is also a literal kingdom.

He is going to extend that rule of God to the ends of the earth, and all the nations are going to come under His government and under the righteousness and justice and mercy of His government. Once we begin to understand that, then we can start to talk about a whole number of other matters.

Kingdom is Kingship

What does this word kingdom mean? Now I have to say straightaway that here in the United States, I am not at all sure that there is any understanding of a kingdom. If only it could say, "The republic of God is going to come," perhaps you would understand a little better. It is very hard for people who have been brought up in the republican tradition to understand kingdom. I am not saying it is wrong, but that is another matter altogether and I am not going into it. The fact of the matter is that a kingdom is a kingdom.

What is this word which is used again and again and again not only throughout the New Testament but throughout the Old Testament? Everywhere you turn you will hear about the kingdom of God and the proclamation of this kingdom. All the prophets spoke of this kingdom of God. It was promised to the kings, particularly David, that this kingdom would be an everlasting kingdom. In one of the greatest empires and in the capital of the greatest empire in the world at the time, God spoke to Daniel about an everlasting kingdom. And it was through Daniel that the Lord said the day would come when the saints shall possess the kingdom. We find it everywhere in the Word of God, but what does the word mean?

For some people, it is a question of territory. They just think of a kingdom as something to do with territory. It is bounded by borders, as it were, and that is a kingdom. It is what we would speak of as the United Kingdom, which does not include the Republic of Ireland. It is England, Wales, Scotland, and Northern Ireland, and its proper name is the United Kingdom of Great Britain and Northern Ireland. And the moment you hear of this United Kingdom, you think of territory. It is not in the North American continent, it is not on the Asian continent, it is not on the African continent; it is the United Kingdom.

However, that is only one aspect of the word kingdom. We cannot understand that every time God uses the word kingdom, He is not talking just about territory, as if He is saying, "The earth is the Lord's and the fulness thereof." There is something far more to the kingdom than mere territory. It is not simply that territory over which the king rules, over which the throne has absolute authority. That is one very important and fundamental aspect of the word kingdom; but actually, we could understand it in another way. It is the throne; and when we speak of the kingdom, we are speaking of the throne, not just a king. Of course, in our connection, it is the King and the only King.

Actually, when we are talking about a kingdom such as the United Kingdom, it could have been ruled by all kinds of kings and queens down through the years. But we are speaking of the throne, of the whole principle of authority, of the whole principle of rule, of a national policy, of a national character, of a national constitution. That is the kingdom. So when we speak and read in the Word of God of the kingdom "Thy kingdom come" it is not only that we are talking about territory, it is not only that we are talking about the extension, but we are talking about the rule and reign of God. We are talking about that constitution, as it were, of God, that constitution that is produced by His purpose, by His Word, and by His will. Mr. Theodore Austin Sparks always preferred another word for this, and I must say that it has helped me more than anything else. He used to substitute the word kingship for kingdom because, in the Greek, it does not just and only mean a territory or even a rule but it is a combination of ideas. He used to say, "Thy kingship come," and "Fear not, little flock, it is the Father's good pleasure to give you the kingship." If you begin to understand it like that, suddenly, a whole lot of things begin to fall into place. "Seek ye first the kingship of God and His righteousness and all these things shall be added unto you." For me, it is not absolutely the best word, but at least it does bring us much nearer to the heart of this whole meaning of the word kingdom.

Kingship is the rule and reign of God and the character of God in His reign and rule, as well as all that He reigns over. Once we begin to see that, then we have the beginning, the first glimmer of an understanding of this whole matter of the kingdom. You will see immediately that if you and I have an argument with the kingship of the Lord Jesus, then we can talk until we are blue in the face about the kingdom of God but, actually, we are living in contradiction to it. If you and I are not prepared to surrender to the kingship of God, if we are not prepared unconditionally, unreservedly to commit all that we are and all that we have to that kingship, it is no good talking about the coming kingdom. It is no good saying how wonderful it will be when the kingdom comes if the kingship of God has not first come to us, if you and I have not come literally, relevantly, practically under His kingship.

The Satanic Challenge to God's Kingship

This matter of the kingship of God, the kingdom of God, lies at the root of world history. Actually, the whole of world history, either negatively or positively, is related to the kingship of God. All recorded history is the record of a satanic challenge to the kingship of God. This explains history. It explains why man, with all his genius and with all his creativity, always falls short. Every time he seems to be bringing in a new golden age, a new Utopia, it turns to ashes in his hands and becomes a prison house, a dungeon.

From Genesis 1 to Revelation 22, we discover this matter of dominion, of authority, of kingship, of kingdom. When God first created Adam and Eve, almost the very first words He said to them were: "Have dominion." And in that amazing Psalm 8, we have almost a prophetic revelation from God concerning His whole purpose for man. This is how it goes:

What is man that thou art mindful of him?
And the son of man, that thou visitest him?
For thou hast made him but little lower than God,
and crownest him with glory and honor.
Thou makest him to have dominion over the works of thy hands;
thou hast put all things under his feet.
Psalm 8:4–6

Right at the very beginning of world history, right at the very beginning of the creation of the universe, we find within the heart of God a purpose for mankind. It is not only that you and I should come under the kingship of God but that we should exercise the kingship of God. But another has entered the arena and that other has challenged God and poisoned mankind, and the challenge is totally to the kingship of God. Wherever we turn, we find this enemy of God. From Genesis 3 right the way through to Revelation 20 we find the story of this great adversary of God, this great enemy of God. And in Isaiah 14, there is a prophetic word concerning Lucifer.

> *And thou saidst in thy heart, I will ascend into heaven, I*
> *will exalt my throne above the stars of God; and I will sit*
> *upon the mount of congregation, in the uttermost parts*
> *of the north; I will ascend above the heights of the clouds;*
> *I will make myself like the Most High. (vs. 13–14)*

Whatever academic problems you may have, here is a revelation from God that, at the very beginning, a poison entered into mankind. How it happened, how it was permitted, why is another matter; but the fact remains that into this world came a poison and a challenge to the kingship of God. Wherever we turn in the whole Bible, we find that we have the record of this challenge.

> *Who delivered us out of the power of darkness and [transferred]*
> *us into the kingdom of the Son of his love. Colossians 1:13*

What a word "Power of darkness." We are born into that power of darkness, born with links to that power of darkness, born with chains that chain us to that power of darkness; and only when something happens to us and we are saved by the grace of God are we delivered from that power of darkness and transferred into the kingdom of God's dear Son.

I think of those other mysterious words where Jesus referred, not once but again and again, to the prince of this world. That is a very interesting title prince of this world. He did not just call him an impostor, He said, "The prince of this world." That speaks of some authority, some kind of status. It is a challenge.

I think of another word from the apostle John. He said these words by the Spirit of God that must surely be almost fathomless in their meaning but which explain so much in world history:

The whole world lieth in the evil one. 1 John 5:19

This is where we all began. I don't care who you are or what you are, what kind of family you came from Jew, Gentile the fact of the matter is we all began here. We all began in this darkness. We all began in this bondage. We all began here until God, by His grace, shone into our hearts and delivered us out of this power of darkness and transferred us into the kingdom of His dear Son.

The Ages-Long Conflict

I think of that wonderful cry in the book of Revelation. Whatever interpretation we may give to it, what a wonderful cry it is:

*And the seventh angel sounded; and there followed great
voices in heaven, and they said, The kingdom of the world
is become the kingdom of our Lord, and of his [Messiah]:
and he shall reign for ever and ever. Revelation 11:15*

*Now is come the salvation, and the power, and the kingdom
of our God, and the authority of his Messiah: for the
accuser of our brethren is cast down, who accuseth them
before our God day and night. Revelation 12:10*

Here we discover that little you and little me are introduced into
a conflict we hardly understand. By the grace of God we have
been saved, and we suddenly find that we have been catapulted,
as it were, into an enormous conflict. We hardly understand the
dimensions of this conflict. We hardly understand exactly what
it is all about except that the moment a person is saved by the
grace of God, they find all kinds of things come out against them.
Every kind of thing is going to try and trip them up. Why should
it be? You have sided with God. Surely everything should be a
bed of roses. Everything should be absolutely right. You should be
carried on beds of ease into the kingdom of God. But no, we find
it is as if the whole world is against us.

"Through many tribulations we must enter into the kingdom of
God" (Acts 14:22b). Why this tribulation? Why all this opposition?
Why this antagonism, unless the enemy cannot bear anybody who
has been transferred? He cannot bear the thought that you have
been taken out of his authority and placed under the authority
of God and of His Messiah. When you begin to understand that,

it makes sense to the whole conflict, an age long conflict, an ages–long conflict.

At the very beginning of the Psalter there is a Psalm that both rabbis and church scholars have called a Messianic Psalm. I am sure you all know it very well.

Why do the nations rage, And the peoples [imagine] a vain thing? The kings of the earth set themselves, And the rulers take counsel together, Against the Lord, and against his [Messiah], saying, Let us break their bonds asunder, And cast away their cords from us. He that sitteth in the heavens will laugh:

The Lord will have them in derision ... Yet I have set my
king Upon my holy hill of Zion. Psalm 2:1–4, 6

What a Psalm! It is a window into an ages–long conflict beginning in Genesis and ending in the book of Revelation. You and I are in it by the grace of God; and if we are in it, not because we are anything in ourselves but because we belong to the Lord Jesus, then victory is assured if we will only come under His kingship. We are invincible if we come under the kingship of God. But if we have an argument with the kingship of God, if we have an argument with the kingship of the Lord Jesus, then we shall find, saved though we shall be, we lose everything. We do not come to the throne; we do not come to kingship in our own lives. We have lost our inheritance but not our salvation.

My dear friends, I find this an unbelievable Psalm. What does it mean? Many times I have thought to myself: "Why do the nations rage? Why do the peoples imagine vain things?" I live in a part of the world where it is exactly true. They are unbelievable with their vanity, all around us, screaming things. It has no sense, it makes no sense, it does not have any relationship to the truth. What is wrong with them? What nonsense! Why all this turmoil; why all this conflict? But it is something to do with the kingship of God. It is something to do with the kingdom of God. It is something to do with the King of God, God's King, God's Messiah.

Isn't it wonderful that the Lord laughs? I love it. He laughs. We get all upset and bothered with everything, wanting to build deep shelters and store up food and all the rest of it for all the things that are coming; but the Lord laughs. He has them in derision. "Yet I have set my king upon my holy hill of Zion." The purpose of God is established. God's King is in His place. Nothing can reach Him or touch Him or overthrow Him, and we are in the train of His triumph.

How stupid we are! Instead of realizing that we are in the train of the triumph of God's King, God's Messiah, who is at the right hand of the majesty on high, we have arguments all the time; we have to be dragged into the will of God. God has to go to the most amazing ways of manipulating us to get us to do even simple things that are His will. Isn't it sad? And if you are thinking of somebody else, why don't you think about yourself because that is true of all of us. We sit there thinking: "Oh, I hope so and so is listening to this. They need it." But in actual fact, we are all stupid when it comes to it. We spend our time arguing with the Lord, misreading God's purpose and word for us, misunderstanding His way for us, misunderstanding His motives in leading us. It is amazing. How clever the enemy is to have injected a poison into us that we need to be clear of, but so often we allow it to remain within our lives, within our circumstances, within our homes, within our relationships. And thus, Satan has ground. We are not like the Lord Jesus when He said, "The prince of this world comes and he has no ground in Me." Would to God we could say such a thing: "He has no ground in me."

God's Program is on Time

Every single thing in the divine program is, at present, on time. It is not a minute behind nor a minute before; it is all on time. I think that is absolutely amazing. It gives me enormous comfort at a time when we could be very confused and when I know many believers are even more confused than I am. There is no confusion with the Lord. Everything that is happening in this world is on time. It is absolutely according to the divine program. Praise the Lord!

That gives me courage to believe that when the time comes which no man knows, neither the angels, nor even the Son of Man, but only the Father, for the Son to begin His journey back with the kingdom of God, it will be on time not a minute before, not a minute behind. It will be absolutely on time.

This present world situation moves toward a world government. I don't have any doubt about it. I know many people are very confused by what has happened in the Soviet Union. They have always thought that the Kremlin was the antichrist and that, somehow or other, that was the power, military power, that was going to cover the whole earth and bring the persecution in Russia, Eastern Europe and China to the whole world. Now suddenly, it is all breaking up. So many believers write to me or telephone me and say: "Don't you think it is a fraud? Don't you think Mr. Gorbachev is just blinding everybody and he is going to suddenly attack the United States?" It is possible because Mr. Gorbachev, whatever you think about him, is still a Communist and a dedicated Communist. But the fact of the matter is this: The Soviet Union has no money. It has no money at all. Do you think they wanted to get out of Eastern Europe? Do you think they wanted to get out of Afghanistan? The point is God, just as with Nebuchadnezzar, has spoken the word and the whole thing is in the process of breaking up; and now believers are all confused.

What about the antichrist? Where is the antichrist going to come from? Well, the antichrist may come from a place and from a source that may surprise you. I don't know where the antichrist is going to come from. I have some suspicions. All I know is this: What has happened started in Poland; it went from Poland to Hungary, from Hungary to Bulgaria, from Bulgaria to Eastern Germany, from Eastern Germany to Czechoslovakia, from Czechoslovakia to Romania; and suddenly, within a few months, the whole of Europe was free. For the very first time ever, Romania televised a whole Christmas Eve service to the whole nation. For the first time in seventy-one years, the Kremlin allowed a Christian service to be televised throughout the whole of the Soviet Union on the Orthodox Christmas Eve and allowed the bells of the Kremlin to ring in the New Year.

What we are witnessing is something amazing because it is going to move to a world government. The Western world has got to do something, somehow or other, to bring in some kind of peace for the world and to stop the possibility of war. It would be foolish for me even to predict, but one thing I am quite sure of: God's program is on time. I don't have any doubt that the emergence of the EEC, the Common Market, as the biggest single force in the world has already begun. And now the great question is: Will Eastern Europe be included? Will Hungary, will Czechoslovakia, will Poland, will Yugoslavia actually be included in this mammoth new United States of Europe?

It is amazing to see all that is happening. On the one side, for the first time, the gospel is being preached in the streets in Prague. The president of Prague is a friend of one of my friends, and when they were in prison together, he prayed every day with him in the exercise hour in the prison yard. He is a believer. And the prime minister of Poland is an observant, committed Catholic believer. It is unbelievable what is happening.

My dear friends, there were two nations in this world that were empowered and inspired by a pagan spirit in the beginning of the thirties. One was Japan and the other was Germany. Both of them spoke of a new world order Japan for Asia, Nazi Germany for Europe. And both of them sought, by military means, to bring that new world order into being Adolph Hitler with his Reich of a thousand years, and Japan with its master race. They were both pagans, and both of them were defeated. Then we have witnessed the most amazing thing: They have become almost the supreme economic powers in the post Second World War period. Now it seems as if these two nations are once again poised, not to take the world by military means, not even to be nationalistic; but the same pagan spirit is permeating, as it were, through them to try and influence the whole of world society. When the United States could not shore up Eastern Europe and the Soviet Union with money because of her weakness in that way, she called upon Germany to do something. But Germany could not do something because she is more interested in reuniting with Eastern Germany, and so Germany called in Japan. When the prime minister of Japan came, he went first to Bonn before he went to all the Eastern European capitals, and he gave the most amazing speech that, in days to come, will probably be one of those watershed speeches. He said, "We are on the brink of a new world order."

My dear friends, I may be wrong in much of what I have said, but at least I think I am right in this. Something is happening like an enormous convulsion in the whole of world society, both in Asia and in Europe. Everywhere we see the turmoils of this society; and as always with these great convulsions, these great shakings, these great turmoils and tumults, out of it will come beasts. It has always been in the history of the world. Why? Because it is a satanic challenge. It is fallen man that wants to bring in a satanically inspired, demonized Utopia, a golden age without God and without God's Messiah. Now I may be wrong on the details, but upon that matter, I think I can be absolutely dogmatic. This is the challenge.

One of the most amazing things is that, suddenly, in the midst of all this turmoil, in all this convulsion, in all this change that has taken place, something is happening among the Jewish people. When I was here last year, I had no idea at all about any of this shows I am no prophet and I don't suppose most of you did either. We have all been taken by surprise by the whole thing. I come from a little nation with enormous problems, facing huge crises. And in the midst of it, at the time most inopportune, at the time when everything, humanly speaking, should cancel out any such possibility, the greatest immigration in our history is taking place. There have been 1,115,000 Soviet Jews who have applied for visas to come to Israel. But it is not just that. Suddenly, 10,000 Ethiopian Jews have applied for visas; 10,000 Romanian Jews have applied for visas, 2,000 French families have applied for visas. It is as if God is breathing upon all the Jews not the ones in America, but upon all the rest and suddenly, something is happening and they are coming back home. It is unbelievable. We haven't got the homes for them nor the jobs for them. We have got the most impossible economy and a bureaucracy that is Eastern European in its spirit. Do you know the Bible says there will come a day when an exodus will come from the north country that will eclipse the exodus from Egypt? If you had asked me when it would happen, I would have said, "Not yet." We have a hopeless economy; we have a very weak government. We've got threats from the president of Iraq about incinerating us and gassing us. God laughs in the heavens; He has them all in derision. He speaks the word to the north, "Give up," and they give it up. He speaks to the south, "Keep not back," and they keep not back. And it all happens. Surely that means only one thing: The kingdom of God must be near. Everything in the divine program is on time. This is no mistake.

I have known believers, Christians, who are non-Jewish, who have gone to the Soviet Union trying to get these folks to come and it has been like hitting their head on a brick wall. They did not want to come. They are so assimilated that most of the men are not even circumcised. In Jerusalem, they are circumcising sixty a week. They don't know the first thing about Jewishness, about Passover or anything else. They don't understand what we are talking about. They never wanted to come back. If they wanted to go anywhere, it was to the United States. This was the promise land. Then God blew on it all. Suddenly, it all happens. It has to be that God is in this thing.

God Has Never Given up His Original Purpose

I have talked about a challenge to the kingship of God. We have said something about the meaning of the word kingdom; but now consider the good news. I am always rather sad about this word gospel. Sometimes we associate it with a kind of soul music. Many people who have not been brought up in Christian circles associate it with barnstorming preachers or fraudulent preachers who preach the gospel and then send the plate around. Others think of it as just something that is not quite right. But gospel means "good news" the good news of God's kingship, the good news of the kingship of God, of the kingdom of God.

What is this good news? I am only going to touch on this because in the next time I want to talk about it more fully. God has never given up on His original purpose to have His King in His place, His kingdom on earth. Did you hear that? God has never given up on His original purpose for His King and for His kingdom. No matter if the whole world is demonized, no matter if all the nations become a fury of antagonism, God has never given up; nor has He given up on His original purpose for man to share in that kingship. He has not thrown in the glove. He has not seen what a mess mankind is. He has not given up over the difficulties He has with believers. My dear friends, every one of us is a nuisance. I have always had the greatest sympathy with Moses, and one day I am going to tell Moses how thankful I am the Lord chose him to lead the people of God through the wilderness and not me. I wouldn't have just broken the stick, I would have broken the rock as well. I get so irritated with God's people at times. I know I am a nuisance, and I have to continually remind myself I am a nuisance to God. It is amazing to me that the Lord loves you and me so much that He saved us, nuisance and all. This modern type of gospel preaching almost sounds like a kind of election: Please vote for the Lord for president. It is a kind of loose, superficial thing. It is not the gospel that we find here in the Book which proclaims that God is King, and the only right way to approach God is with humility and repentance. That was the gospel preached in the beginning. But in spite of this, we get the idea that we are doing the Lord a great favor by siding with Him. "He should be so pleased. He should fall over Himself doing everything for us because we have given up everything, you know. Just to go with Him is not so popular." What a difference it is to that old-time gospel preaching in which people wept for hours over their sins, wept over their lost estate, and wept their way into the kingship of God. God did such a deep work in lives that, somehow or other, they were delivered from pride at the very beginning of their Christian lives, broken at the start, understanding that it was the grace, mercy, and favor of the Lord that had saved and that, by saving us, the Lord has only introduced a load of trouble to Himself. Any child of God who thinks that they are doing the Lord a great favor in following Him, does not know anything about the gospel of the kingdom.

God Will Establish His Kingdom on the Earth

God has not given up on His original purpose, not only to have His King, not only to have the kingdom but to share that kingship with others. He intends to establish His kingdom, His King and those who will reign with Him. Isn't that wonderful?

The kingdom of this world has become the kingdom
of our Lord and of His Messiah and He shall
reign forever and ever. Revelation 11:15b

Then I think of that wonderful little chapter, Isaiah 2. I always remember this because when I was first saved at twelve years of age and had never read the Bible, nor been in a place of worship, I remember being told if the Bible ever repeats something, it is very significant.

And it shall come to pass in the latter days, that the mountain of
the Lord's house shall be established on the top of the mountains,
and shall be exalted above the hills; and all nations shall flow
unto it. And many people shall go and say, Come ye, and let
us go up to the mountain of the Lord, to the house of the God
of Jacob; and he will teach us of his ways, and we will walk
in his paths: for out of Zion shall go forth the law, and the
word of the Lord from Jerusalem. And he will judge between
the nations, and will decide concerning many peoples; and
they shall beat their swords into plowshares, and their spears
into pruning–hooks; nation shall not lift up sword against
nation, neither shall they learn war any more. Isaiah 2:2–4

These words are repeated word for word in Micah 4. This is the purpose of God to establish His kingdom on the earth. It is a literal kingdom that is coming. He is going to decide over the nations. It is not just to do with the saved; it is to do also with the nations of the earth. God is going to vindicate His truth ultimately before all the nations.

I think of another wonderful Scripture, just as remarkable in my estimation, in Isaiah 11 which speaks of the Lord Jesus, God's King.

And there shall come forth a shoot out of the stock of Jesse, and a branch out of his roots shall bear fruit. And the Spirit of the Lord shall rest upon him, the spirit of wisdom and understanding, the spirit of counsel and might, the spirit of knowledge and of the fear of the Lord. Isaiah 11:1–2

And the wolf shall dwell with the lamb, and the leopard shall lie down with the kid; and the calf and the young lion and the fatling together; and a little child shall lead them. And the cow and the bear shall feed; their young ones shall lie down together; and the lion shall eat straw like the ox. And the [suckling] shall play on the hole of the [viper], and the weaned child shall put his hand on the [cobra's] den. They shall not hurt nor destroy in all my holy mountain; for the earth shall be full of the knowledge of the Lord, as the waters cover the sea. Isaiah 11:6–9

What a prospect! That is the purpose of God, to establish this. Here then is the good news. God has, already, His King. That King is Jesus, God's Messianic King, born of the royal seed, born according to the prophecy, in Bethlehem Ephrathah, according to that word:

> But thou, Bethlehem Ephrathah, which art little to be
> among the thousands of Judah, out of thee shall one come
> forth unto me that is to be ruler in Israel; whose goings
> forth are from of old, from everlasting. Micah 5:2

Here then is God's King. He was born King of the Jews. Wise men came from the East inquiring, "Where is He that is born King of the Jews? You know the story. People sometimes speak of the humanity of the Lord Jesus in a quite false way. They speak of Him as a peasant, as some kind of an artisan. It is true, He was a carpenter. He grew up in very humble, pressurized circumstances, but there was not a drop of blood in His veins that was not royal. He was the King. When He came forth for His public Messianic ministry, He was acclaimed everywhere; and I don't know whether most people who read their Bibles without background to it would understand. You remember blind Bartimaeus and what he said? "Son of David, have mercy upon me." Why did he call Him Son of David? Why not Son of Man? Why not rabbi? Why Son of David? It came again and again and again. People said, "Son of David." It was as if they were saying, "Crown Prince, Crown Prince." They knew it was Jesus. They knew that He was of the royal seed, that He belonged to the tribe of Judah, that He was of the royal house of David, that He was David's greater Servant.

If the chief priests and that ecclesiastical mafia had really wanted to destroy Jesus, they could have said to people: "Come to the registry and we will prove to you that this Man is not royal,

He is not of the royal seed. We have all the genealogical tables extant." They never once mentioned it. What they did say to Pilate was, "He says He is a king." And when Jesus was crucified, there was only one title nailed above His head. They could have put, "Jesus of Nazareth, Savior of the world"; it would have been right, but they didn't. They could have said, "Jesus of Nazareth, Prince of peace"; but they didn't. They could have put, "Jesus of Nazareth, He said He was the King of kings and Lord of lords"; but they didn't. They put, "Jesus of Nazareth, the King of the Jews."

When God raised Him, He vindicated His Messiahship and His Kingship. This means that at the right hand of God stands the King, Head of the church, King of kings and Lord of lords, ruler of the kings of the earth, and still King of Israel. That is why He returns to Jerusalem. I have never had an adequate explanation as to why Jesus is going to return to Jerusalem where, at the present time, there are less believers than in any of the capital cities of the world.

God has His King; that is good news as far as I am concerned. That is good news because this King is a Savior. This King is not some great king exhibiting His royal majesty, exhibiting His royal power, dressed in all the regalia, wanting to be admired and looked at, as so often people on this side of the Atlantic imagine kings. "Wonderful, marvelous; I would love to be a king, sitting there with nothing to do, with an orb in one hand and a crown on my head." Some people have got the idea that is what it is going to be in the kingdom to come. You are going to have an orb in one hand and a sceptre in the other, a crown on your head and you can hardly move. You will just be sitting there on a throne while all the angels admire you. It is so stupid.

The Biblical idea of kingship is service, it is servanthood. The King is the servant of the Lord. That is the character of kingship. And that is why, when you and I begin to see Jesus in this way, we discover He is not just some potentate, some majestic personage who has an aura of mystery around Him. This is the One who washed His disciple's feet. This is the One who loved them to the end. This is the One who knew that Judas was a swindler and still loved him. This is the one who loved you and gave Himself for you. My dear friends, there is nobody else in the whole world who is more worthy to sit upon God's throne. Here is a character of kingship that means utter humility, utter brokenness, absolute service. God has His King. Praise His holy name.

Kings and Priests Unto God

The second thing is that God intends to share this kingship of Jesus with others. Now I want to put a word of warning in here. Jesus is unique. I have known Him now for quite a few years, and I find the Lord Jesus absolutely unique. I do not want to take away from the Lord Jesus. I shudder sometimes when I hear the Lord Jesus spoken of as a thing, as if He is an "it"; as if He is only a life, a power, an agency, an instrument. This marvelous Lord Jesus is a Person. It is amazing to get to know Him, to walk with Him, to hear Him. This Jesus is unique; but God still intends to share His kingship with others. It is said of Jesus, in the letter to the Hebrews, that He shall bring many sons unto glory. We have been made priests kings and priests unto God. Isn't that wonderful!

This is good news. I think it is absolutely marvelous. Here am I, a rotten little troublemaker, as far as God is concerned.

I don't think I try to make trouble with you, but as far as God is concerned, I am a troublemaker. I am always troubling Him. Poor Lord, I feel so sorry at times. I misunderstand Him, I misread Him, I misinterpret Him. Sometimes, He has to whack me with His rod; sometimes, he has to lift me up. What a lot of trouble I am to that wonderful Lord. But He intends me to be a king. I can hardly believe it. He wants me to come to His throne isn't that amazing? To share His throne and sit with Him on His throne, not, as I have said, in some way to be admired but, with Him, to administer the purpose and will of God in the ages to come. I find this amazing.

The City of God

I would like to stop and talk about the city of God. That is the very last thing in the whole Bible, and the capital city is all to do with government and authority and the executing of national policy. That bride is the city; isn't it amazing? Look at the Bible: It begins with a wedding Adam and Eve and it ends with a wedding the Lamb and the wife of the Lamb. And in the midst of it is two little books that most people don't really understand. Little theologians call one of them a bawdy love ditty. One is called Ecclesiastes and the other is called the Song of Songs.

In Ecclesiastes you find, if you believe the Jewish tradition, Solomon did everything and he said: "Vanity, vanity, all is vanity. Emptiness, emptiness, all is emptiness. Uselessness, uselessness, all is uselessness." And some Christians say, "I don't think this book should be in the Bible." It is the most amazing book. It says not to be too righteous and not to be too wicked because in the end you are going to die anyway. This is not like the rest of the Book. Even the rabbis argued and argued and argued about the little book of Ecclesiastes: "Should it be in, should it not be in, should it be in, should it not be in." And finally, they said it should be in.

But the Song of Solomon is altogether different. If we understand the Jewish tradition, it was a vision God gave to Solomon of the love between God and His covenant people. The whole thing is an education. God takes that girl and delivers her and brings her into a relationship with Himself. Then she becomes complacent; and He leaves her. Then she goes out to find Him, and when she finds Him, she is in a deeper level. Then He leaves her again and she goes out to find Him, and in the end they are forever together.

Vanity, vanity, all is vanity; uselessness, uselessness, all is uselessness that is the book of Ecclesiastes. Solomon ought to know. He built parks, he had zoos, he had botanical gardens, he had farms, he had palaces, he had a thousand wives; he ought to know what he was talking about. But when we come to the Song of Solomon, value, value, all is value; purposefulness, purposefulness, all is purposefulness. It is here in the heart of your Bible. The Bible begins with a wedding, it ends with a wedding, and in the middle of your Bible is a wedding. What is it all about unless it is that God longs that you and I should come to the throne of the Lamb, as if He longs that you and I should share in the kingship of Jesus, that we should be those who could reign with Him? My dear friends, that is good news.

By the Grace of God

How can we get there? Not by our works, not by our zeal, not by our devotion, not by our religious knowledge, but by His grace. That is the good news of the kingdom. This Lamb gave Himself for us. This King became the sin-bearer. This Jesus is the One through whom you and I are justified in the sight of God, declared righteous, given an eternal foundation so that you and I can become kings with Him. That is good news. Not only has He saved us but He has provided us with the wherewithal, the power, the wisdom, the grace that you and I should not only be saved but that we should come to the throne of God. Here then is the good news of the kingdom. Jesus went everywhere preaching this good news of the kingdom. It turned His known world upside down. And it is interesting that in that great discourse on His second coming, it is said that this gospel of the kingdom shall be preached in all the nations in the whole world for a testimony to all nations, and then shall the end come.

My dear friends, isn't it an amazing thing that you and I have been saved? I think it is such a privilege in these days of confusion, of turmoil, of convulsions, of so much that is happening that you and I, by the grace of God, have been saved. It is the grace of God that we stand in His presence. We have entered the race, we entered His school, we have entered His education, His discipline. This is good news, as far as I am concerned. May the Lord make it true to us all.

Shall we pray?

Beloved Lord, we need that spirit of wisdom and revelation in the knowledge of the Lord Jesus to be granted to us. We have been considering this whole matter of the gospel of Your kingdom. Lord, let that shaft of divine light shine right into our hearts. Bring us to a new understanding of this amazing position that You have brought us into, this amazing status that You have given us. You have saved us with an everlasting salvation. You have justified us in Your sight through the work of the Lord Jesus at Calvary. Dear Father, for us, it is good news. Now bring that home to every one of us that we might begin, in a new way, to understand what it is in this world which, Lord, is so filled with ideas contrary to Your truth and to Your Word. Bring us to a new place of understanding and bring us to a new experience of Your kingship. Lord, help us, we are so foolish; we argue with You, we rebel against You, we often misunderstand You altogether. Lord, deal with us in love and in mercy that we may be those who come absolutely under Your kingship, especially in these days. We ask it in the name of our Lord Jesus. Amen.

2.
It Is All of His Grace

Luke 4:42–43

And when it was day, he [Jesus] came out and went into a desert place: and the multitudes sought after him, and came unto him, and would have stayed him, that he should not go from them. But he said unto them, I must preach [the gospel] of the kingdom of God to the other cities also: for therefore was I sent.

Luke 8:1

And it came to pass soon afterwards, that he went about through cities and villages, preaching and bringing the [the gospel] of the kingdom of God, and with him the twelve.

Luke 16:16

The law and the prophets were until John: from that time the gospel of the kingdom of God is preached, and every man entereth violently into it.

Shall we pray?

Father, as we turn to You, we want, in the light of Your Word and the ministry of Your Word, to confess our absolute need of You, both in speaking and in hearing. Lord, we have no other plea and we have no other foundation. We have no other righteousness than the Lord Jesus; and in Him, we come to You, Father. By faith, we stand into all the glorious enabling power and grace that You have made available to us through the finished work of our Lord Jesus. Will You open Your Word to us so that it is not just a word of truth for the mind but, Lord, it may be that word of life that is deposited within our beings. We commit ourselves to You over this very important matter of the kingdom of God, and we ask it in the name of our Messiah, the Lord Jesus. Amen.

My responsibility in this wonderful theme "Thy Kingdom Come" is "The Gospel of the Kingdom," that good news of the kingdom of God that Jesus Himself preached and which, in Himself, Jesus brought. This good news of the kingdom of God is all of His grace. From beginning to end, it is all the grace of God. Its foundation is the grace of God, its top stone is the grace of God, our introduction into this kingdom is by the grace of God, our reaching the goal of this kingdom is by the grace of God; and every development within it, every step taken by faith, every new discovery of the Lord Jesus, every new experience of His power and of His fulness is by the grace of God. This is the gospel of the kingdom.

I have no idea why it is that in Christian circles this word gospel seems to have been reduced to something very introductory, something, we could call almost kindergarten.

They have called it a "simple" gospel. The Scriptures speak of no such thing. It is described again and again and again as the gospel of the kingdom of God and I believe that is the missing note in our gospel preaching. We take simply the facts of the gospel Jesus was born, Jesus died, Jesus has won salvation, Jesus offers forgiveness (which, of course, is tremendous). But the early church proclaimed, first and foremost, the kingship of God and, on that basis of God's absolute sovereignty, declared the truth concerning God's Son and then demanded, commanded repentance. That is something far, far more than so much gospel preaching that we are used to today.

You Must Be Born Again

I know when I say that this gospel is all to do with the grace of God that some people will almost immediately turn me off. They will say: "This is not to do with the deep things of God. This is all kindergarten. This is going to be all very initial, so I might as well have a sleep." But in my estimation, this whole matter of the grace of God is absolutely fundamental. It is fundamental not only to our entrance into the kingdom of God but to every single stage in its development. Every single thing to do with the kingdom of God touching this earth, coming into our lives, coming into our circumstances, coming through the church into communities, into localities, affecting the nations is all to do with the grace of God, the sovereign grace of God. You remember that amazing talk that Nicodemus, one of the great rabbis of his day, had with the Lord Jesus in the night.

Jesus answered and said unto him, Verily, verily, I say unto
thee, Except one be born anew [born again], he cannot see the
kingdom of God. Nicodemus saith unto him, How can a man be
born when he is old? can he enter a second time into his mother's
womb, and be born? Jesus answered, Verily, verily, I say unto
thee, Except one be born of water and the Spirit, he cannot enter
into the kingdom of God. That which is born of the flesh is flesh;
and that which is born of the Spirit is spirit. Marvel not that
I said unto thee, Ye must be born anew [again]. John 3:3–7

God Has Done the Impossible

This second birth is something beyond fallen man in himself.
The greatest scientists cannot produce a second birth. The greatest
doctors of medicine cannot produce a second birth. The greatest
doctors of theology (and we have many of them) cannot produce a
second birth. Only the grace of God can bring a man or a woman
to a second birth. Whoever a man or woman is, whatever their
background, whatever their cultural context, whatever their
pedigree, or lack of it, only the abounding grace of God can bring
them to the kingdom of God. And once we begin to see that,
we begin to understand why in this same chapter in this talk with
Nicodemus, Jesus went on to say:

And as Moses lifted up the serpent in the wilderness, even so
must the Son of man be lifted up; that whosoever believeth
may in him have eternal life. For God so loved the world,
that he gave his only begotten Son, that whosoever believeth
on him should not perish, but have eternal life. John 3:14–16

The good news of the kingdom is that God alone has done the impossible. What is impossible to fallen man, what is impossible to the best of fallen man, to the most educated of fallen man, to the most religious of fallen man whether he is bad or good, ignoble or noble God has made possible through His grace. Fallen man, man born of Adam however clever, however resourceful, however knowledgeable, however gifted, however religious is barred from the kingdom of God.

Do you remember when man fell right at the very beginning of the record of the Word? God set cherubim at the tree of life with a flaming sword lest men seek to enter into the kingdom of God and become recipients of God's eternal life in their fallen state. It is a picture of something tremendous. In other words, God put a veto on fallen man. You can have your League of Nations, your United Nations. They can talk about golden millenniums and utopias. They can seek with this ideology or that ideology or this philosophy or that philosophy or this political system or that political system to try to bring peace on earth and unity and prosperity and love; and every one of these great attempts ends in bondage, in corruption, in wickedness, in enslavement, in evil. God has put a veto on Adam and all that are in Adam. He has put a veto on us. We are barred from this kingdom; the gates to this kingdom are closed.

Flesh and Blood Cannot Inherit the Kingdom of God

When we look at some of the Scriptures in this matter, they almost make a shudder run through us.

Now this I say, brethren, that flesh and blood cannot inherit the kingdom of God; neither doth corruption inherit incorruption. 1 Corinthians 15:50

Did you hear that? We hear this at every funeral service, normally, and it goes in one ear and out the other. You have to be born of the Spirit. Only that which is born of the Spirit can inherit the kingdom of God. Only that which is declared righteous by God Himself on the basis of the finished work of the Lord Jesus can enter into the kingdom of God.

Flesh and blood is a very comprehensive term. He is not saying, as some people, especially those with Hellenistic ideas, tend to think: "Flesh, oh yes, flesh is always evil; flesh is bad. If only we could be rid of the flesh. If we could say good-bye to the body, if somehow or other, the physical could be laid to one side, then we should be pure." Satan himself does not have flesh, but nobody thinks of that. It is a Hellenistic idea that by getting rid of the body, by getting rid of the physical, we become pure. This is one of those unbelievable things that seeped into the whole theology of the church and has influenced everybody so that we get this idea that flesh is evil. But my dear friends, this flesh and blood can be so good, so noble, so religious, so devoted, so zealous. It can know the Bible from Genesis to Revelation, but it cannot inherit the kingdom of God. It is only when we are born of the Spirit. It does not mean that when we are born of the Spirit, we lose our flesh; of course not. It may have to be crucified. God may have to do something; but, in the end, our entire spirit, soul and body will be preserved entire unto the coming of the Lord Jesus. So here we have a very comprehensive term.

This is not talking about flesh and blood which is Hitlerite, flesh and blood which is Stalinist, flesh and blood which is Mao Tse-tung, flesh and blood which is all that is dark and ignoble and base. This is flesh and blood which includes Shakespeare, Goethe, and Schiller. It includes all the great poets, all the great painters, all the great composers with all their magnificent gifts to mankind. This is flesh and blood which cannot inherit the kingdom of God, not because God does not like the creativity that is in us, not because God does not like the genius that He has placed within us but because there is a poison in fallen man which can never be trusted not now, nor in the age to come. There is a divine veto on that kind of man because he is never safe. So we have here an amazing Scripture; it is very comprehensive.

Now most people understand only these kinds of Scriptures:

Or know ye not that the unrighteous shall not inherit the
kingdom of God? Be not deceived: neither fornicators,
nor idolaters, nor adulterers, nor effeminate, nor abusers
of themselves with men, nor thieves, nor covetous,
nor drunkards, nor revilers, nor extortioners, shall
inherit the kingdom of God. 1 Corinthians 6:9–10

We are more acquainted with this kind of flesh and blood. Anyone who is sensible understands straightaway this kind of flesh and blood cannot inherit the kingdom of God. But then we turn to Galatians 5 and we get something more of a shock.

Now the works of the flesh are manifest, which are these:
fornication, uncleanness, [that comes nearer to many]

lasciviousness, idolatry, sorcery, enmities, strife, jealousies, wraths, factions, divisions, parties, envyings, drunkenness, revellings, and such like; of which I forewarn you, even as I did forewarn you, that they who practise such things shall not inherit the kingdom of God. Galatians 5:19–21

When we take a good look at this kind of thing, if we are honest with ourselves and face the facts, we are barred from the kingdom of God. Even if we felt that there was no jealously in us, if we felt there was no party spirit within us, if we felt there was no partiality within us, if we felt there was no uncleanness in mind or thought or heart, still we are flesh and blood. We are fallen flesh and blood, self-centered flesh and blood, egocentric from the moment we enter this life. And upon us, there is a divine veto.

We Are Born Again to an Inheritance Incorruptible

Let me put it another way: Only those who are as righteous, as pure, as holy, as perfect as the Lord Jesus can enter the kingdom of God. I am going to say that again. This is the gospel that ought to be preached, normally. Only those who are as righteous, as pure, as holy, as perfect as the Lord Jesus can enter the kingdom of God and inherit it. Doesn't this disqualify us all? We are disqualified. Now if you begin to see this, you will understand the good news of the kingdom of God. I am disqualified that is not good news. But I am disqualified; it doesn't matter what I do. I can live like a hermit; I can go, like some of those dear men used to, up on the top of a pole and spend my whole life sitting there trying to make myself holy. I can wall myself up in a cave a little way from my home, as many of them did in days gone by, to try and make myself acceptable for the kingdom of God. But according to this Book, unless I become as righteous and as pure and as holy and as perfect as the Lord Jesus, I am vetoed, I am barred, I am disqualified. Yet God has called us to His kingdom and His glory.

To the end that ye should walk worthily of God, who calleth you into his own kingdom and glory. 1 Thessalonians 2:12

Faithful is he that calleth you, who will also do it. 1 Thessalonians 5:24

Wherefore, brethren, give the more diligence to make your calling and election sure: for if ye do these things, ye shall never stumble: for thus shall be richly supplied unto you the entrance into the eternal kingdom of our Lord and Saviour Jesus Christ. 11 Peter 1:10–11

How can we have this rich supplying of this entrance into the kingdom of God's eternal glory? How can we know this? How can you and I actually come to the kingdom and not just into the kingdom but come to the throne of God within that kingdom? How can you and I be educated and finally qualified for the kingship of God? There is only one way: "By grace have ye been saved through faith; and that not of yourselves; it is the gift of God; lest any man should boast" (see Ephesians 2:8). Did you hear that very simple gospel word? It is the gift of God. He saves us through His grace. But He does not merely save us;

He begets us. This is the good news of the kingdom. He begets us. He actually brings us to a new birth, to a second birth. It would be marvelous if we were saved but minions in the kingdom of God. It would be marvelous if we were eternally saved just to be subjects in His kingdom. But He does far more than just save us, He begets us again. In other words, He becomes Father to us. He actually brings us to a second birth whereby you and I are born of the Spirit and qualify for inheriting the kingdom of God.

> Blessed be the God and Father of our Lord Jesus Christ [the Messiah], who according to his great mercy begat us again unto a living hope by the resurrection of Jesus Christ [the Messiah] from the dead, unto an inheritance incorruptible, and undefiled, and that fadeth not away, reserved in heaven for you, who by the power of God are guarded through faith unto a salvation ready to be revealed in the last time. 1 Peter 1:3–5

This is such a wonderful word that it just runs off us like water off a duck. We get so used to these wonderful words: "Begotten again unto a living hope by the resurrection of Jesus Christ from the dead, unto an inheritance incorruptible, undefiled, and that fadeth not away." My dear friends, does the good news of the kingdom of God begin to dawn on you? If you have put your faith in the work of the Lord Jesus and in the Person of the Lord Jesus, you, by the grace of God, have not only been merely saved, delivered from the power of darkness, transferred into the kingdom of God's dear Son, you have been born again by His Spirit to an inheritance incorruptible, undefiled. In other words, this inheritance cannot fall; it cannot be spoiled; it cannot be compromised; it cannot be corrupted; it does not fade, as most things do in this world, from its initial glory. It is an inheritance incorruptible, undefiled, that fadeth not away, reserved in heaven for you. I say this is something unbelievable.

"Who by the power of God are guarded unto that salvation." My dear friends, isn't it marvelous, we are saved, we have been saved, we are being saved and finally, we shall be saved? Actually, the full consequences of our salvation are all reserved. It is wonderful just to think about it in a moment, a new body like unto His, a likeness to the Lord Jesus. Think for a moment of all the consequences of this salvation. It is reserved for us this inheritance. "By the power of God are guarded unto a salvation ready to be revealed at the last time."

We Stand by the Grace of God

I have no doubt why the Lord Jesus called this good news. It is a tragedy that most Christians are basically unaware of this. This whole thing is relegated to an evangelistic meeting and the result is that multitudes and multitudes of believers, of Christians truly born of God do not understand their salvation. They do not understand that grace lies at its foundation. They do not understand that every movement forward is by the grace of God. Every discovery of God is by the grace of God. Every new experience of the Holy Spirit is by the grace of God. I am told by Christian psychiatrists that it is a very sad fact that a very large number of psychiatric patients are evangelicals and charismatics. Isn't that interesting? And I will tell you why: When a person becomes a believer, they suddenly take on a standard far,

far greater and higher than anything they ever had when they were unsaved; and being saved by the grace of God, they know the love of God, but they feel God is always making discoveries about them. They feel that, suddenly, the Lord said this morning, "Oh, I had no idea so and so was so rotten." And so we say, "I cannot come into His presence, I cannot speak with Him because He has discovered something about me." Actually, He has not discovered anything about you; you have discovered something about yourself, that is all. As if the Lord did not know how rotten you were! Do you know that every one of us, subjected to certain circumstances, to certain situations, to certain temptations, would undoubtedly fall? Not one of us would stand but by the grace and the power of God. The only way that you and I can possibly stand is by the grace of God.

God Is Father to Us

For ye received not the spirit of bondage again unto fear; but ye received the spirit of adoption [placing or recognition], whereby we cry, Abba, Father. The Spirit himself beareth witness with our spirit, that we are children of God: and if children, then heirs; heirs of God, and joint-heirs with Christ; if so be that we suffer with him, that we may be also glorified with him. Romans 8:15–17

What a salvation! We are not merely saved to be a subject or a minion in the kingdom of God, not merely born again of His Spirit and brought into a family, the family of God but the Spirit of the Lord is shed abroad in our heart, establishing a practical, relevant, living day to day experience with the eternal God, the Most High. The Spirit is shed abroad in our hearts crying "Abba, Father."

Many Christians suffer; they do not know this relationship in practice. For them, God is still a distant schoolmaster. He is some huge disciplinarian. If I may be so irreverent to describe it, but it is true of many believers, He is some kind of divine capitalist who has an enormous factory in which He works everybody to death. How few believers know the Fatherhood of God! How few believers appreciate the Fatherhood of God! And I am not talking about being familiar. I have heard people call God "Papa"; I think it is terrible. The Holy Spirit may be shed abroad in our hearts with this marvelous relationship, but God is still God. But we have a relationship with Him. He is Father; He is "Abba" to us.

The Work Jesus Did on the Cross

Only those whom God justifies are subjects of His kingdom and members of His family. Did you hear that? Only those whom God justifies are subjects of His kingdom and members of His family. But how could God break the hold which the power of darkness holds us with? How could He sever the link between us and a satanized and fallen mankind?

I wonder whether most believers have ever really begun to understand Calvary. Sometimes, preachers dwell on the physical sufferings of the Lord Jesus on Calvary, and we do not underestimate them or devalue them; but the fact remains that Jesus only suffered physically for six hours. It is a most remarkable fact that the gospels do not dwell on His physical sufferings.

We hear His cries, we hear the conversation, we hear the jeering of the crowds; the facts are given to us in an almost journalistic way. In fact, it is almost as if the gospel writers are so conscious of a fathomless mystery that they dare not talk merely about the physical. You have to go to the Old Testament to actually understand something of the agony of the One on the cross. In Psalm 22, you have the most unbelievable account of Calvary from the eyes of the One on the cross. But it is the untold story and the untellable story that is the real suffering of the Lord Jesus. I always take a few Scriptures and I go for a journey with those who are with me through those Scriptures. It is the only way I know of being able to communicate something of that work that the Lord Jesus did on the cross.

All Sin Was Laid on Him

All we like sheep have gone astray; we have turned every one to his own way; and the Lord hath laid on him the iniquity of us all. Isaiah 53:6

In the Hebrew, the word is, "He has made to gather on Him the iniquity of us all." That is not just sin but the most depraved word for sin, the sin that speaks most of the abominable depravity of sin from Adam right the way through all the great figures of history; all the iniquity of every single person ever known Adolph Hitler, Stalin, Mao Tse-tung came upon the Lord Jesus. Into one single human frame was compressed the iniquity of the whole world from its beginning to its end.

Behold, the Lamb of God, that taketh [beareth]
away the sin of the world! John 1:29

There is nothing more beautiful than a lamb, nothing more innocent, nothing more sweet. Always, to all people all over the world, whatever culture, a newborn lamb is a symbol of innocence, of purity, of righteousness. But then we have a most amazing thing. "And as Moses lifted up the serpent in the wilderness, even so must the Son of man be lifted up" (John 3:14). Now a snake is exactly the opposite. It is a symbol of all that is dark, of all that is cunning, of all that is deceitful. It is a symbol of the underworld, it is a symbol of the name of Satan. It is everything that is poisonous, everything that is horrifying. Now we suddenly find that this Lamb of God upon the cross became the uplifted serpent; as if, into Himself, He took the very poison of Satan, as if He took into Himself that venom which has poisoned the whole of mankind and barred us from the kingdom of God.

And Jesus saith unto them, All ye shall be offended:
for it is written, I will smite the shepherd, and the
sheep shall be scattered abroad. Mark 14:27

He is quoting the prophet Zechariah, but the prophet Zechariah didn't say that. He said, "Smite the shepherd, and the sheep will be scattered." In the Hebrew, it does not say, "I will smite the shepherd;" nor in the Septuagint version, which is the Greek version of the Old Testament the early church used. So why did the Lord Jesus change this word, unless He was seeking to bring home to us that it was not Satan that struck Him, it was not even mankind Jew or Gentile that struck Him; it was God Himself who struck His own Son. When the Lamb became the uplifted serpent and all iniquity was laid upon Him, God struck Him; and out of the darkness, out of His tortured heart came the words, "My God, My God, why hast Thou forsaken Me?"

He Tasted Death for Every Man

We know not what happened in those hours except that Jesus tasted death for every man, not in just a general way. It is beyond our minds, it is beyond computation that He tasted death as if it was your death and He tasted my death as if it was my death and He tasted death for every man. In that moment, Jesus died with those words "Finished."

And the veil of the temple was rent [torn] in two
from the top to the bottom. Mark 15:38

We shall never understand what happened to the Lord Jesus, neither now nor in eternity. I do not care how long eternity is it is endless none of us with our finite minds, even all of us together, will ever understand all that the Lord Jesus went through. But this we know: He won our salvation. He came back with a finished work, with a salvation of God which breaks the link between us and satanized humanity and brings us to the place where we can be delivered from the power of darkness and transferred into the kingdom of God's dear Son. This is indeed good news. Could there be anything more wonderful? I think of the old hymn:

All my sin, not in part but the whole, is nailed to His cross, and
I bear it no more. Praise the Lord, praise the Lord, oh my soul.

In Isaiah the Lord said, "I have blotted out as a thick cloud thy transgressions." And in another place, the Lord said, "I will remember your sins no more." How could this be; in what way? This is how the Spirit of God described it to the apostle Paul:

Him who knew no sin [God] made to be our sin ... that we might
become the righteousness of God in Him. II Corinthians 5:21

Did you hear that? He who knew no sin (that is the Lord Jesus) God made to be our sin (your sin, my sin) that you and I might become the righteousness of God in Him. I was disqualified from the kingdom of God; how is it possible for me to become the righteousness of God? It is only when God justifies me on the basis of the work of the Lord Jesus. For my sin was not only canceled, it was not only blotted out, it is not only remembered no more, it has been transferred. Upon Jesus' perfect frame, all my sin was placed, and His righteousness was transferred to me so that God says, "Lance is righteous." Can you believe that? Now you know me well enough to know that it is not possible if God did not say, "I declare him righteous on the basis of My Son's finished work, for My Son became Lance's sin that Lance might become My Son's righteousness." This is what it means to be justified just as if you had never sinned.

It is such good news that most believers cannot believe it is as simple as that. They say: "Oh, no, no, it is going too far; this is extreme, this is radical. If it goes on like this, we would all be able to live in sin." But this is the good news of the kingdom of God. Of course, you cannot live in sin. But the fact of the matter is this: Here is a foundation. The foundation of God's kingdom is the grace of God. It is the finished work of the Lord Jesus.

Humility–Repentance–Faith

Now I make a most amazing discovery. I find that in Romans it says that the gospel, the good news of God is the power of God unto salvation to every one that believes; to the Jew first, and then to the Gentile (see Romans 1:16). Or I think of 1 Corinthians where the apostle puts it, again, in a slightly different way. It is the same idea.

> For Christ sent me not to baptize, but to preach the gospel: not
> in wisdom of words, lest the cross of Christ should be made
> void. For the word of the cross is to them that perish foolishness;
> but unto us who are saved it is the power of God ... But unto
> them that are called, both Jews and Greeks, Christ the power
> of God, and the wisdom of God. 1 Corinthians 1:17–18, 24

Here then we begin to understand the good news of the gospel. How can you and I enter into this kingdom of God? Only when we humble ourselves. There is none of this kind of presidential election atmosphere that is so often found in so many of our evangelistic meetings. We sell Jesus as if He is a commodity; we devalue Him, we make Him all sweet and sentimental, we make Him appealing, we make Him popular; and then we ask people to vote for Him, to put up their hand. I am not saying you cannot be saved by putting up your hand or by standing up. I came to the Lord when I stood up in a meeting. I thank God for such a challenge, but the fact remains that this gospel is not some presidential election. It is not some appeal to you to throw your weight behind Jesus. It is not some appeal to you, somehow or other, to vote for Him. It is not an appeal to you to do Him good, to put your energy and your gifts at His disposal. This gospel is that you and I need to humble ourselves before God and repent from all our dead works. We are to turn away from our sins. If there was more old-fashioned conversions, with people weeping over their sin, we would not have the immorality we have in the church, we would not have this superficiality in the church, we would not have all this worldliness in the church because men and women would have, at the very heart of their experience, repentance. And this is the gospel. Look anywhere in the whole New Testament and you will find it was the same with every apostle, every evangelist: "Repent and believe on the Lord Jesus." Humility, repentance, faith the three essential constituents if you and I are to be saved, if you and I are to be born of God.

All God's Dealings in the Kingdom Are by Grace

Listen carefully, because this comes home to us as believers. The foundation of all God's dealings with us from the day you and I are saved, from the day we are born of God is the same grace and the same finished work of the Lord Jesus. Only if we humble ourselves can we go on. That is why God abominates pride. Where there is pride of any kind, it bars us from any progress in the kingship of God. It frustrates the purpose of God in our lives. I have seen people come into an experience of the Holy Spirit that has changed their whole life, and I have seen other devoted believers who have not. These devoted believers come to me and say: "So and so is a ragtag person; they are just no good. There must be something wrong with this whole matter to do with the Holy Spirit. This so and so is absolutely nothing; and yet he comes into a real experience of the Holy Spirit. I have been serving the Lord for years and years and years and I don't." There is no humility. And not only no humility but, my dear friends, I will tell you something else: You are trusting in your zeal and in your devotion and in your work, as if that will win God's favor and bring you into a deeper experience of the cross or a deeper experience of the Holy Spirit or a deeper discovery of what the church is. It is so simple.

I find it terribly hard; I don't know about you. You see, the foundation for God's kingdom is grace. So I feel: "Well, I am a Jew. I think I have a better chance than you. After all, these people are my relatives." I feel like the apostle Paul did: "I have a claim on You, Lord. These others here are good folks; they have been saved, but they are only Gentiles. I am a Jew, Lord." But the Lord does not do anything. Then I see someone who is a Gentile, and not just an ordinary Gentile. He comes from a family of convicts; he has a past of nothing but bad and delinquency in his life. Then he begins to see and enter into fulness. And I say: "What is wrong? Here am I. My mother came from the tribe of Benjamin, my father came from the tribe of Judah, one of the great Jewish leaders is one of my relatives. Here am I, Lord; what is wrong?"

The basis of all God's dealings in the kingdom of God is His grace, not your pedigree, not your background, not your knowledge, not your zeal, not your good works; it is the grace of God. From beginning to end, if I am going to know what it is to be crucified with Christ, only God can reveal it to me and only by His grace will He reveal it to me, for no other reason. If I am to know the Holy Spirit in all His indwelling, the fruit of the Spirit, it is only by the grace of God I shall know the work of the Holy Spirit. If I am to know the anointing of the Holy Spirit with all His gifts and all His power it is only by the grace of God that I will know such an anointing. Further, if I am to see what the church is and practically be in its building up, related to other brothers and sisters, then it will only be by the grace of God. When you think about it, this is good news. If it really was a question of pedigree, if it really was a question of our background, if it really was a question of our studies, if it really was a question of our zeal, where would we be? No, my dear friends, here we have something so marvelous that I say this is the good news of the kingdom of God.

Many, many years ago, God gave a vision to a certain Hebrew prophet called Zechariah. It was all to do with the testimony of Jesus. It was to do with the building program. Zechariah was so burdened. Everything seemed to be going wrong, and then God showed him this seven branch menorah, this lampstand and the two olive trees. Then came the word,

Not by might, nor by power but by my Spirit saith the Lord of hosts. Who art thou, O great mountain? before Zerubbabel thou

shalt become a plain: and his hands shall bring forth the top
stone with shoutings of Grace, grace, unto it. Zechariah 4:6–7

The work began in the grace of God, it developed by the grace of God, and it would end by the grace of God. Here then is the good news of the kingdom of God. Any man or woman who finally comes to the throne of the Lamb, who finally overcomes and sits down with the Lord Jesus in His throne, who is part of that bride, of that city that will reign with Him forever, it will be all of grace. May the Lord bless every one of us and this preaching of the gospel. May it reach our hearts.

Shall we pray?

Father, we want very simply to respond to You. We take this matter to do with Your grace and the gospel as so kindergarten; and yet, Lord, so few of us understand it. When You begin to deal with us and when You begin, as it were, to disturb us and turn us upside down and inside out, then Lord we become neurotic, nervous, full of accusations and charges from the enemy. Oh Lord, let this gospel of the kingdom get into our hearts this day, and may we know that whom God justifies, who can accuse? Lord Jesus, work in our hearts in the most wonderful way to open the eyes of our hearts, to understand in a new and fuller way than ever before this matter of the gospel of the kingdom. We ask it in the name of our Lord Jesus. Amen.

3.
Suffering Violence

Luke 16:16

The law and the prophets were until John: from that time the gospel of the kingdom of God is preached, and every man entereth violently into it.

Matthew 11:12

And from the days of John the Baptist until now the kingdom of heaven suffereth violence, and men of violence take it by force.

Shall we pray?

Heavenly Father, we thank You as we come into Your presence and turn to Your Word that You have made available to us all the energies and powers, all the grace and wisdom of our Lord Jesus in the Person of the Holy Spirit. And we want to avail ourselves of that anointing both for my speaking and our hearing that this time may not be misspent, neither be in vain, but Lord, we may meet with Thee and receive from Thee. So together, by faith, we stand into all the provision that You have made for us for this time. Make this time live with Your presence, with Your working, with Your speaking, Lord. And we shall give to You all the praise and all the glory in the name of our Messiah, the Lord Jesus. Amen.

On this matter of the gospel of the kingdom, I sought to introduce the subject in the first time, and in the second time, we spoke about the grace of God as the foundation of that kingdom. I want to take this matter one step further, and I want to start with this very strange statement of the Lord Jesus about the kingdom of God suffering violence and men of violence taking it by force. It must seem a very strange statement to many people who think of Jesus as gentle, meek, and mild. They might almost wonder whether someone misquoted it or misinterpreted it; but here we have it, not only in Matthew's gospel but also in Luke's. The way Luke records it is that every man entereth the kingdom of God violently.

Now I find this very interesting because there is a common (and I think erroneous idea) about the gospel very prevalent in Christian circles, both evangelical and charismatic that it is really a very simple matter. It is just something to do with the forgiveness of God and a kind of conversion. But actually, the gospel of the kingdom is infinitely more. When we look at the Acts of the Apostles, we find a very interesting thing. We find this phrase again and again. It says, "And Paul preached the kingdom of God"; or it says, "Preaching and teaching the kingdom of God." We discover that this gospel, this good news of God's kingdom, of God's kingship is far more than merely being forgiven. That is the initial thing. But the fact of the matter is that this gospel, the presence of this kingdom of God, the preaching of this kingdom of God, the presence and preaching of the kingship of God always challenges people. There is no way that the kingdom of God can be present or preached and not challenge men and women. It confronts us. It confronts us with realities. It confronts us with eternal realities. It forces us to decisions. It is not merely to do with salvation nor even only with accepting the kingship of God, the kingship of the Lord Jesus. It is also a question of our kingship, of our being educated, trained, disciplined, brought by spiritual growth to the place where we can administer the will of God, where we can come to the throne of God.

This is the good news of the kingdom of God. Therefore, this matter of the gospel of the kingdom has very much to do with character lasting, eternal, genuine character. It has very much to do with experience, real and genuine experience of God. It has very much to do with growth, spiritual growth to maturity, genuine growth to maturity. It is not just growth in the head, in academic knowledge, in a kind of theology but a growth within our very being in both experience and in character.

Required Violence

We will look at this matter in three ways, all of which are related. The first thing I want to underline in this matter of the good news of the kingship of God is the required violence. Violence is required if you and I are going to reach the goal of God's kingdom, if you and I are going to come to the end of the Lord. If you and I are going to realize the very significance of the gospel for us, then you and I are required to exercise violence. In Luke 16:16, it says,

"The gospel of the kingdom of God is preached, and every man entereth violently into it." I do not think this means that your new birth is violent. What I believe it means is this: that you can only enter into the kingship of God in experience. You and I can have that character of kingship produced in us which will bring us to the throne of the Lamb, bring us to the throne of God only if we are prepared to be violent. Now we have to be violent not with one another, as is so often the case in Christian circles, but violent with one's self.

This word violence is interesting because most of us mollycoddle ourselves. We wrap ourselves up in cashmere and silk; we beautifully care for ourselves. What we feel others should go through, the way they should be disciplined is something quite different to the way that we look after ourselves. But every man can only realize the end of the gospel, the goal of the gospel if he enters into this matter violently.

In Matthew 11:12, we have it put perhaps even more clearly: "The kingdom of heaven suffereth violence, and men of violence take it by force." Now there is no getting away from this. It is not as if, somehow or other, this word violence has very unfortunately got into the record and should not really be there. We are told quite clearly the kingdom of heaven suffers violence. This kingship of God suffers violence, and men of violence take it by force. You cannot get away from that. No amount of theological acrobatics will enable us to get out of this matter. Here there is a required violence. Only those children of God, born of God's Spirit, who are prepared to be men and women of violence can take this kingship of God. It has to be taken by force.

Apparently, it is not enough to believe in the kingdom. Every child of God that I know who has had a real experience of the Lord Jesus believes in the kingdom, but there are very few children of God I know who have kingship in their character. Now why? It is not just a matter of sitting there apathetically, almost indifferently, impartially, and saying: "I believe this; I believe in the coming kingdom. Thy kingdom come. Oh, it is going to be wonderful when the Lord comes, when the Messiah comes and His reign extends to the ends of the earth. How wonderful, how marvelous it will be." It is not just a question of believing in some kingdom. It is a matter of taking some kind of action.

It seems to me, if I am honest with myself, and I am sure it is the same with you, that there is a deep resistance in us to the kingship of God. Even though we are saved, even though we are born of the Spirit of God, even though we believe in the Word of God, still there is within us a deep resistance; and unless you and I are prepared, spiritually, to use violence with ourselves, there is no way forward. There is no way you and I are going to enter into the kingship of God. There is no way you and I are going to come to the throne of God. There is no way that we are going to submit to the discipline of God, to the education of God, to those tribulations and afflictions that will come our way in God's school of kingship. We have to be violent with ourselves. The goal of the gospel, the aim of God for His kingdom will never be realized without such violence on our part.

Lay Hold On

I want to take you to the apostle Paul's Philippian letter to a reasonably well-known verse:

> *Not that I have already obtained, or am already made perfect: but I press on, if so be that I may lay hold on that for which also I was laid hold on by Christ Jesus. Philippians 3:12*

I think this word lay hold on is a very interesting word, and I imagine that most of us do not really think of it in the way that we ought to think of it. Actually, in Greek, it is the word for a policeman arresting a criminal. But the old King James version uses that word apprehend. Now when you apprehend someone, it is not just sort of getting to know them as some people imagine. Apprehend is when a hand is laid on your shoulder and you are arrested by an officer of the law. You are apprehended. Now that is old English. Very sadly, of course, here in the United States, when you seceded from England, you also seceded from the English language. One comes up, again and again, against problems in English with English English and American English. I always remember a little caption I saw on the New York Times when I first came to the United States many years ago: "English is the language which divides the United States from the United Kingdom."

Apprehension: "That I may apprehend that for which also I was apprehended by Christ Jesus." Let's put it another way: "That I may arrest that for which I also was arrested by Christ

Jesus." Let's put it another way: "That I may lay hold on that for which I also was laid hold on by Christ Jesus."

I thank God that, in my little life, the Lord Jesus took hold of me violently. He took hold of me when I had no idea of Him or what He was or who He was or anything. I had never even read the Scriptures when I was twelve years of age. I had never been to synagogue nor to chapel nor to church, but I remember that day when the Lord Jesus took hold of me. Now when He first took hold of me and I saw the Lord, I had no idea what it all meant; I did not understand. I just knew, somehow, that He was alive, that He was real, that He was the Messiah and He was the Savior; that was all I knew. I had no idea that when He took hold of me, it was for a purpose. It was years afterward I began to discover that it is not just to be drab, little, anemic, colorless Christians, sitting in rows in meetings looking at one another, waiting until we grow toothless and blind and, finally, we shall be transported into some heavenly kingdom where we shall be part of an eternal choir forever and ever and ever and ever and ever.

This kind of gospel that is being preached, which has brought this whole matter into disrepute, is so sad. It is so limited, it is so destructive. It is absolutely true, there is nothing more wonderful than to be forgiven; there is nothing more wonderful than to know your sins are cancelled, blotted out as a thick cloud. There is nothing more wonderful than to be saved, to be delivered from the power of darkness and transferred into the kingdom of God's dear Son; but that is not the end of the matter. God has a purpose for you and for me. When the Messiah Jesus took hold of you, it was with a glorious destiny in mind, with a glorious purpose in mind, with an unbelievable goal in His heart.

He took hold of you, but if you do not exercise violence and take hold on that for which He took hold on you, you will never come there. I am not saying you will not be saved. I did not say that. I am not saying that you lose your salvation. I am not saying that you lose your place in the kingdom of God. God is so gracious and so loving. But if you and I are not prepared by the Spirit of God, by the grace of God, by the work of the cross to lay hold on that for which also we were laid hold on by Christ Jesus, we will miss the mark: saved, but not in the throne.

We sang a little Scripture song a few days ago about there being no more tears there; it will be tearless there. But you know, my dear friends, I am sorry to have to tell you that the Scripture says there will be tears there, not all the time, but it says God will wipe away all tears. I have often wondered why we will cry. Will it be just the relief for being there? Will it be the wonder of finally being in the presence of God that causes us to burst into tears? Could it be that for some of us, it will be regret that we misspent time, lost opportunities; that we never, by violence, laid hold on that for which also we were laid hold on? We are saved, but we have not reached the end of the Lord.

Count It All Loss

When I read the apostle Paul, I find it so unbelievable. This greatest of all our rabbis, this man who spoke of himself so clearly in this testimony (the most remarkable testimony I think in the Bible), this man who said that to be a Jew was in every way to have value, said here in this testimony, "I count it all loss for the excellency of the knowledge of Christ Jesus my Lord." Here is a man who was not just preaching a truth, he was manifesting it. Here is someone who had truly exercised violence with himself. He was laying hold on that for which also Christ Jesus laid hold on him. I think that is worth a lot of reflection and meditation.

Fight the Good Fight

Of course, it is not only there. In the first letter of the apostle Paul to his son Timothy we read these words that sadly, most Christians only know in hymn form: "Fight the good fight of the faith, lay hold on the life eternal, whereunto thou wast called" (1 Timothy 6:12). It is not just coasting along, it is not just being carried along, it is not just drifting in some kind of spiritual relaxation, some passive current of the Spirit of God, just being passively carried along by the power of God. Here is the word of the apostle at the end of one of his last letters to his beloved son in the faith, Timothy: "Fight the good fight of faith, lay hold on life eternal, whereunto you were called." In other words, what the apostle is saying is this: "My son, Timothy, you stand to lose everything but your salvation if you do not fight the good fight of faith, if you do not lay hold on that life eternal to which you have been called."

I sometimes wonder whether many of us do not experience resurrection life, eternal life, the life of God in the Lord Jesus because we don't lay hold on it. We seem to think we are the recipients of eternal life and that is all that matters. It is there; but we have to lay hold on it. We have to, by faith, stand into it. We have to fight the good fight of faith.

Many Christians, as we have already made reference to, are fighting another kind of fight. Very often, it is a fight with one another. Everywhere I go, in Christian work and in fellowships, I find people fighting with one another. It is not a good fight; it is fighting the bad fight. This is a fight of faith. Fight the good fight of faith.

Now this isn't just a one time matter. If you look in Timothy, we have exactly the same thing again.

> *Laying up in store for themselves a good foundation against the time to come, that they may lay hold on the life which is life indeed. 1 Timothy 6:19*

> *I therefore so run, as not uncertainly; so fight I, as not beating the air: but I buffet my body, and bring it into bondage: lest by any means, after that I have preached to others, I myself should be rejected. 1 Corinthians 9:26*

He, of course, is not talking about salvation; he is talking about an inheritance. He is talking about the kingship; he is talking about the throne. And he is saying here, in this unbelievable little window into his heart: "I don't run in an uncertain way. I am quite clear as to what the goal is. I don't box (that is the word in Greek) the air. I am doing it in a way that I am bruising my body; I am actually disciplining my body." This is the same thing. It is this whole matter of violence.

Who Can Be Saved?

In the gospel of Matthew, this is all capsulated in one little statement that has always intrigued me. Do you remember when

Jesus said that it was impossible for a rich man to enter the kingdom of God, and then He used an unbelievable illustration. He said it is as impossible to push a camel through the eye of a needle as for a rich man to enter into the kingdom of God (see Matthew 19:24). Now this sounds like good radical, revolutionary talk. I always think camels are most extraordinary creatures. I have a fondness for camels. I always remember a brother who told me a camel is a horse put together by a committee. I don't agree. I think the camel is one of the most remarkable creatures in the world; and when people tell me this creature evolved, I just can't believe it. I can only believe that someone with immense humor created the camel. And here is the Lord Jesus talking about a camel, that great dromedary camel with the one hump, not the Bactrian camel of China and Central Asia with the two humps which is smaller. Can you imagine trying to push that camel through the eye of a needle?

Now some people say this eye of the needle was a little door in one of the gates of Jerusalem that they used to take the camels in when they came late; but they had to take everything off the camel to allow the camel to go through. You can discount it. No Jewish merchantman would ever leave his goods outside of the city wall and take the camel inside. You can forget that altogether; it is absolute nonsense. He transported them hundreds of miles; now he leaves them outside where brigands and robbers are. These Christian interpretations are unbelievable. The fact of the matter is, if you take a little needle and you look at the eye of the needle and you look at a camel with that wonderful face; you could not even get the snout of a camel through the eye of a needle. Can you imagine? Oh, the humor of the Lord.

Can you imagine people getting a camel and pushing it and pushing it and pushing it and, somehow, trying to get it through the eye of that needle? It is impossible. Then the Lord brought home the punchline. No more can a rich man enter the kingdom of God, or the kingship of God, than a camel can go through the eye of a needle. Immediately, we think, "Oh, we know what the Lord is talking about; He is talking about riches." It comes just after the story of the rich young ruler when Jesus said: "There is only one thing you lack. Go and sell all that you have and come, follow Me"; and he turned away sorrowfully. But Peter and the other apostles understood something far more than just a question of a literally rich man because Peter said, and apparently the others assented with him, "Then Lord, who can be saved?"

Now Peter was not a rich man. I have stood in Tiberius in Capernaum by the Lake of Galilee by Peter's little home. They discovered it some years ago. That home is very small. It was the first house church in Galilee. It was there that Jesus stayed in one little tiny room. He was not a rich man. It is possible that Matthew was a rich man because he was a tax collector.

Most of them were pretty wealthy because they took bribes on the side and they became quite wealthy. John came from a very good family, but Peter and Andrew were very poor. Here was Peter saying, "Then who can be saved?" He had understood something. It was not just a matter of world; apparently, it was self-sufficiency, any trust in yourself whether it is in your intellect, whether it is in your ingenuity, whether it is in your resources, whether it is in your personality, whether it is in your background, whether it is in your pedigree, whether it is in your property, whether it is in your professional status. It does not matter what it is; but if you trust in those things, it is impossible for you to come into the kingdom of God.

Now do you understand what it means: "The kingdom of heaven suffereth violence and men of violence take it by force"? There is something within us that resists this kind of thing. Why should I let go of my intellect? Why should I let go of my ingenuity? Why should I let go of my natural resources? Why should I let go of my pedigree? Why should I let go of my professional status? Why should I let go of my money, if that is what I trust? It needs violence.

The Inescapable Cost

The second thing I want to consider on this matter to do with the gospel of the kingdom is the inescapable cost. This is the complement to all I said about the grace of God because the Lord Jesus did everything required for you and me to enter the kingdom of God, and that foundation of His finished work and of His grace remains forever. There is no way to enter the kingdom of God, no way to progress in the kingdom of God, no way to reach the throne of God but by that grace of the Lord Jesus. But it would be entirely false of me if I were to leave you with an idea that the gospel does not cost. This is the missing note in modern gospel preaching. Whenever the Lord Jesus preached this gospel, wherever He preached it, though He healed the sick and raised the dead and cleansed the leper, He confronted men and women with the inescapable cost of the kingdom of God. My dear friends, you can be saved, you can be born of the Spirit of

God, but you will not move a step or two in that kingdom unless you are prepared for the cost.

The Lord Jesus spoke of following Him; and somehow or other, in this modern kind of gospel preaching, it seems as if it is a bed of roses. You come to the Lord Jesus and you will be wafted along, blown along, almost catapulted along by some great force. You will not have to do anything, you won't have to pay anything, you will just be taken right the way through to the throne of God. It is not true, for the Lord Jesus said, "If any man come after Me, let him deny himself, take up his cross, and follow Me." This was not some elite luxury experience for special saints. This was His gospel. This was all to do with the grace of God which only can save us, which can only cancel our sins, which can only bring us to a place where we are justified in the sight of God. But then if you and I are going to come to the goal of that gospel, to the end of the Lord in the kingdom of God, then you and I have a price to pay.

Your Self-Life

What is that price? I suggest it is you. It is your self-life, my self-life. If that self-life of yours, that self-life of mine is left untouched, unbroken, undisciplined, uncrucified, it will be our undoing. We can never reach the throne of God unless that self-life is dealt with.

And he called unto him the multitude with his disciples, and said unto them, If any man would come after me, let him deny himself, and take up his cross, and follow me. For whosoever would save his life shall lose it; and whosoever shall lose his life for my sake and the gospel's shall save it. Mark 8:34–35

The Lord Jesus used that word self- life, soul-life, psyche, however you like to put it that life. If I hold on to it, I lose it; if I lose it, I find it. This is the inescapable cost that is involved in the gospel of the kingdom.

Then said Jesus unto his disciples, If any man would come after me, let him deny himself, and take up his

The Gospel of the Kingdom cross, and follow me. For whosoever would save his life shall lose it: and whosoever shall lose his life for my sake shall find it. Matthew 16:24–25

And he that doth not take his cross and follow after me, is not worthy of me. He that findeth his life shall lose it; and he that loseth his life for my sake shall find it. Matthew 10:38–39

Verily, verily, I say unto you, Except a grain of wheat fall into the earth and die, it abideth by itself alone; but if it die, it beareth much fruit. He that loveth his life loseth it; and he that hateth his life in this world shall keep it unto life eternal. If any man serve me, let him follow me; and where I am, there shall also my servant be: if any man serve me, him will the Father honor. John 12:24–26

In Jesus' preaching the gospel of the kingdom, will you notice that Mark tells us it was not just to an inner circle of very special, elite, superior disciples. He brought the whole multitude together, as if the Lord Jesus was saying, "This is the gospel of the kingdom." If you and I want not only to enter into the kingdom, to see the kingdom but to reach the throne of God, then you and I are going to have to face the cross. It is not very popular in these days, when the whole of our generation talks about rights, to understand that the inescapable cost of following the Lord Jesus means the voluntary sacrifice of your rights. "Let him deny himself, take up his cross and follow me." You must understand that we have the wisdom of hindsight. We know that Jesus died on that cross. So now we look back at these words of His in the light of what happened on the cross. But can you imagine those disciples? You see, it was a very common sight in Jerusalem to see those sentenced to death by the Roman authorities carrying the broad beam of the cross with their sentence hanging around their neck; or if they were slightly more wealthy, a servant would go before them carrying it. But anybody carrying a cross beam was already sentenced to death. They had the sentence of death within themselves; they had no more rights. They were on their way to the execution.

Jesus takes from that kind of picture and He says: "Settle it in your heart. If you are going to understand the gospel of the kingdom, the good news of the kingship of God; if you are going to come to that kingship yourself; if you are going to come as one of His sons to glory; if you are going to come to His throne and sit with Him in His throne, then you have got to settle this matter of rights." This is what it means to deny yourself. It does not mean that heavy kind of religious piety that is just a question of dressing in dark clothes and looking morbid and miserable, singing slow hymns like a funeral march, and having your head permanently bent down with your eyes on the ground. That is religion; that is not the cross of our Lord Jesus.

The cross of our Lord Jesus is the way by which He brings us into life and more life and even more life. The Lord Jesus never spoke of His crucifixion without, in the same breath, speaking of His resurrection. He never spoke of losing your life without finding your life. He never spoke of going down but that God would lift you up in the end. My dear friends, here is the inescapable cost of the gospel of the kingdom.

I want to suggest to you that our problem is very simple: We cannot trust. When the Lord says to me: "Now Lance, you have a very vibrant self-life. You have a self-life which you love. I have noticed from the day you were born that you have loved it very much. You have looked after it; you have cultivated it; you have made it as educated and as sophisticated as you can. You love it; it is your darling. Now if you hang on to that self-life of yours that you love so much, you are going to lose it; but if you will lose it for My sake and the gospel's sake, you will find it." Then I say to myself: "How long, Lord? If I can just put it on the altar quickly and then take it back in an instant, it will be alright, Lord." It would all be over in an instant, like one of these new dental appointments so quick. But once you have let go of that life of yours, there is no telling how long the Lord will leave it down there.

Then comes the thought: "Maybe if I let go of my life for His sake and the gospel's, He will forget me. He will forget me altogether. He will go off to the great people like the Watchman Nees and the really great people who have laid down their lives. He will think of them; but me, He might forget in the busyness of the kingdom.

So I think it is better for me to hold on to it." As we say in an old English saying: "Better the devil I know than the one I don't." So I hold on to that life of mine because it is safe with me. I am in charge of it, I know it exactly, I know all of its faults and failings; but if I hang on to it, it will be okay. My dear friends, you hold on to your life, you lose it; it turns to ashes in your hands. That life that you thought would be so interesting, so full, so vibrant, decays, corrupts; and in the end, it brings you almost to the place of suicide, even as a believer. You are so in despair over your own self-life. No wonder you and I need to exercise violence. There is no other way. But it is not just violence; you cannot exercise violence if you don't have faith. You must really trust the Lord that He wants the best for you and He is going to do the best for you.

Those words that we read of our Lord Jesus in Mark 8 and Matthew 16 were prefaced by a most remarkable incident. It starts like this: And Jesus began to tell them that He would go up to Jerusalem, be rejected of the chief priests, crucified, and on the third day, rise again. Dear Peter; Peter gets all the blame for being impulsive and impetuous but, in actual fact, the Scriptures tell us that all the others said the same; but nobody ever thinks of that. Poor old Peter was one of those people who always opened his mouth and spoke for the rest; then the rest kept quiet and they could all disappear. And Peter was left there, always in trouble. So Peter said, "Lord, never; we are not looking for some Messiah that is going to be crucified, executed on a Roman gibbet. Never! We won't allow it. I will stand there myself, Lord. I will not allow a person to lay a hand on You." These are very sweet sentiments, faithful sentiments, loyal sentiments; and they brought a quite uncalled for response from the Lord Jesus: "Get thee behind Me, Satan; you don't mind the things of God, you mind the things of men."

My dear child of God, if you came to me with such a problem about your self-life and you were saying: "No, I am not going that way; that is not the gospel for me. My gospel is all joy and peace, fulness, satisfaction; and I don't like this thing you are talking about"; and I said to you, "Get behind me, Satan," you would go to a leading brother and say, "I think that was the most terrible thing that any visiting speaker in Richmond has ever said." It is one thing for me to say to you, "I think you are thinking negative thoughts"; or if I were to say to you, "I think that is wrong thinking, the way you are thinking," that is quite pleasant. Or even if I said, "Now be careful, I think Satan is manipulating your mind," even that is nicer. But to look straight in your eyes and say, "Get behind me, Satan," that is a most terrible thing.

Here was a child of God. This child of God, only a few moments before, had said, "Thou art the Messiah, the Son of the living God." And Jesus had said to him, "Blessed art thou, Simon Barjona; flesh and blood has not revealed this to you, but My Father who is in heaven." He had revelation. He was devoted to the Lord Jesus. He had followed the Lord Jesus. He had given everything up to be with the Lord Jesus. And now the Lord Jesus said to him, looking into his eyes, "Get behind me, Satan."

If you and I have an uncrucified self-life, it is the playground of Satan. No matter how noble it is, no matter how cultured it is, no matter how beautiful it is, no matter how educated it is, it is the playground of Satan. There is no way that you and I will reach the throne of God with that unbroken self-life. Satan will see to it. He will let us go a certain way, and then he will play on our circumstances, play on our emotions, play on our feelings until he has destroyed us. That is why Jesus said, "You don't mind the things of God, you mind the things of men." You cannot hold both.

In Matthew's version, it is put like this: "You are a stumbling block to me." Oh my dear friends, how many servants of God I have known (I pray to God that I am not included) who are stumbling blocks to their own ministry, stumbling blocks to the fulfillment of the very ministry and work God has given them to do. I know them all over the world people who have yearned to see something happen, people who have longed to see God work and are themselves, without hardly knowing it, the stumbling block to everything that God wants to do. We are the witnesses (Do I have to go beyond the United States?) to a whole number of ministries, true ministries of God, truly anointed by God in some cases, truly raised up by God but which have gotten into the most terrible mess because of unbroken self-life.

I remember when the Lord met with Moses, and He was going to send him to Pharaoh. He said to Moses, "What is that in your hand?" And Moses said, "Lord, it is a rod." Now what was that rod? Those of you who know your Bible will remember that wonderful Psalm written in King David's youth when he was but a lad: "Thy rod and thy staff, they comfort me." Moses had been a shepherd for forty years; and as so often near where I live, we see the shepherd with his rod. It was as if the Lord said, "What is that?" And Moses said: "It is the emblem of my work, Lord. It is my rod. I could not do anything without this rod." Actually, God was going to use this rod all through Moses' life.

It was the rod that he lifted up over the Red Sea when it parted into two. It was the rod that he pointed at the rock when water came out of it. God used this rod; it was an emblem.

Then God said, "Throw it on the ground; lay it down; lose it." Moses threw it down; and in an instant, that inanimate piece of wood became a viper, a sand viper, in Hebrew, an asp. This is the most poisonous of the sand snakes. Although Moses had lived forty years in the wilderness and forty years earlier in Egypt, the moment he saw it, he fled from it. You do not throw a snake down on the ground without it getting a bit angry, especially a sand viper or a horned viper. As Moses ran, the Lord said, "Moses, come back!" Then Moses turned and said, "Never, Lord, not with that thing on the ground." "Now, Moses, take it up by the tail." The one thing you never do is take up a poisonous snake by the tail. Anyone who has lived in the desert for forty years knows that. You just do not do that. If you do, it will curl around and sting you. What an extraordinary thing the Lord said to Moses: "Throw that rod down." It became a snake.

I can imagine Moses saying: "My goodness, I have had that thing with me beside my bed for the last forty years. I have had it inside of my robe, sometimes, in cold weather. I have whacked sheep with it. I have done all kinds of things with it. I had no idea it was a poisonous snake." And now the Lord says, "Take it up by the tail." I can imagine Moses saying, "Lord, do You really mean it?" And the Lord said, "Take it up by the tail."

Now Moses was a man, and a man's man. I know he was the meekest of all the men on the earth, and people imagine that means he was weak; but he was a hero in the Libyan campaign, the hero of the Ethiopian campaign, and he was decorated by

Pharaoh. He was a man's man. And I can imagine that inside (if I know anything about it) he quaked. But outwardly, he went forward and took the tail and instantly, it became a rod again. This was the rod that was used to bring every one of the plagues of Egypt and the Red Sea was parted by.

Do you begin to understand something? He that loseth his self-life shall find it; and he that holds on to it or seeks to preserve it, will lose it. That poison will kill you if you hold on to it. The only way you and I can come to the throne of God is by laying down ourselves. This is the inescapable cost.

So often in Christian circles, especially in recent years, there has been almost a dichotomy between the work of the cross and the work of the Holy Spirit, as if these two works are in opposition. It is as if an experience of the Holy Spirit is all power, all fulness, all gifts, all joy, all ecstasy, and the cross is all affliction, all heaviness, all brokenness, all darkness. But it is not so. I read the words of John the Baptist in Matthew 3, and I find them very interesting. John described the heart of Jesus' ministry as baptizing with the Spirit just as he described the heart of his ministry as baptism in water for repentance. This is what he said:

I indeed baptize you in water unto repentance: but he that cometh after me is mightier than I, whose shoes I am not worthy to bear: he shall baptize you in the Holy Spirit and in fire Whose fan is in his hand, and he will thoroughly cleanse his threshing-floor; and he will gather his wheat into the garner, but the chaff he will burn up with unquenchable fire. Matthew 3:11–12

Can you get this clear? This grain has a husk and a kernel. Have you got it? It is the same grain. It has a husk and a kernel. The kernel is the value, the chaff is the rubbish. Have you got it? When the Holy Spirit does His work in us, God gets the grain and Satan gets the chaff. He burns it up. Now why is it that we don't understand this in the work of the Holy Spirit, as if the cross can work apart from the Holy Spirit? The work of the cross is a work; the Holy Spirit is a Person. It is the Holy Spirit who takes the work of the cross as fire and burns up everything that is not of God the chaff and gathers everything that is of the Lord to be kept and guarded forever. Now if you begin to understand this, you will understand the inescapable cost.

I firmly believe in experience of the Holy Spirit. There are those who have experience of the Holy Spirit right at their new birth, and I thank God for that. I myself am persuaded that the term baptism of the Spirit covers the whole work of the Holy Spirit, both His indwelling and His anointing, His indwelling and His empowering, if you like. But the fact of the matter is, in these days of superficiality, these days of cheap decision, these days when there is a gospel preached which sounds more like a presidential election campaign than a call to repentance, there are very few people who understand anything about the Holy Spirit when they are saved, just as we did not understand the cross when we were saved. We have to, by the blessed ministry of the Holy Spirit, step by step, come into our understanding.

I can well remember when I first understood that when Christ was crucified, I had been crucified. What a revelation it was! And I can remember the first time I ever understood that the Holy Spirit was in me and upon me. It has been one of the greatest joys in my own little life to get to know the Holy Spirit as a Person. I shudder when I hear people speaking of Him as "it." In the same way, I find it so hard when Jesus is spoken of as a commodity, as an "it," a life, a food. Of course, Jesus is a life; of course, Jesus is food; but He is a Person a Person to come to know, a Person to discover, a Person to experience, a Person to walk with.

Here then is the inescapable cost of the gospel of the kingdom. There is no way to follow the Lord Jesus without the cross. There is no way to know the work of the Holy Spirit and be safe unless we are prepared for the cost. May God help us.

Sacrificial Worship

I don't know how to describe this last thing. I am very nervous, almost, of even touching on it. Our brother Watchman Nee once spoke about it, and it seems to me that one cannot talk about the gospel of the kingdom without touching on that amazing incident when that dear lady brought the most precious thing in her home and household and broke it and anointed Him. In the ancient days, in every Jewish home, people thought a lot about death. In the Jewish tradition, death is always an enemy, never a friend; and I must say, that is how I view it. But the Jew always thought about death. This lady, as far as I can see, was not a wealthy lady, but she had an alabaster vase. We have some of these in the Rockefeller Museum in Jerusalem. They had a stone alabaster stopper and they had some kind of glue that glued them. You bought this to keep for when a relative died or when you died, and then it was broken and used. The poor people in many homes did not have the money to go out when someone suddenly died and buy a whole pound of liquid nard. So they used to buy it in a good day when they had a bit of money; or sometimes, a husband would bring it home as a gift; or sometimes, a relative who came into a little windfall would buy it and give it to his sister or give it to his brother to be kept in the home. This was always stored. And even the alabaster vessel itself was very, very valuable, especially in a poor home.

In Matthew's gospel, chapter 26, and Mark's gospel, chapter 14, we have an amazing story told. There were all kinds of people in and out, talking with the Lord Jesus; and quite a lot of business was going on. Suddenly, this lady appeared with her alabaster cruse. I don't know how she broke it. She would have been careful because she did not want to get splinters in it; but she probably struck it on something, perhaps on the stone floor, and then poured it quickly into a bowl. While Jesus was still talking, she began to anoint His head and His feet; and the disciples were horrified. Judas, in particular, was the most horrified of them all. He said: "This is terrible, terrible. Lord, stop this woman. Do you realize what she has done? She has taken the wages of a whole year and wasted them in this stupid act." Of course, they said, "You know, we could have used this on evangelism; we could have used this on the poor." And Jesus said: "You will always have the poor with you, but you won't always have Me. This woman has wrought a good work. She has anointed Me for My burial."

Of all the eleven apostles, of all those disciples, this dear, almost insignificant woman according to Matthew and Mark we don't even know her name was the only one who understood that Jesus was going to the cross. And she wanted to do something; she wanted to do something that was supreme worship.

She wanted to express an identification with Him, a union with Him, an understanding with Him, if you like, a standing with Him. She wanted to enter into His sorrow in some small way and be with Him.

The rest ate their meal and were satisfied. They had no idea that Jesus was about to die. They discussed little theological details. I have no doubt, if I know anything about believers, they talked about this little point and that: "What did you mean by this? I think he meant this. No, I don't think so. What did Moses say? What did Jeremiah say? What did Ezekiel say?" So the discussion went backwards and forwards. They were totally unaware of the shadow of the cross. But this one little lady, by the Spirit of God, understood.

Now you must understand our culture. In the Jewish culture, women are very free; not like in some other cultures, where women are bound. As they do in Chinese homes, women have a very remarkable and amazing position in the household. But they cannot push their way in when the men are present. Now do you begin to understand? She could not just come in and say: "Lord Jesus, I want to have a word with You. I understand where You are going. I want You to know I am with You." She could not do that. So into her heart came an idea: "While they are all talking, I will bring my alabaster cruse and break it and anoint Him. They won't understand, but He will."

This is the character that comes to the throne. This is the kind of person that the Spirit of God has dealt with and made sensitive, has given an understanding to that the others never have. Their heads can be filled with theology, their heads can be filled with Scripture, their heads can be filled with all the activities so necessary in the life of the church and the work of God; but this woman had a heart that understood. I say that is the sacrificial worship which has to be the end of the gospel.

I think of the apostle Paul and that marvelous word: "I beseech you therefore, brethren, by the mercies of God, to present your bodies a living sacrifice, holy, acceptable unto God, which is your spiritually intelligent worship" (Romans 12:1). Here was this dear sister, this dear lady who had never been to seminary; probably, she had never been to school. Yet she understood more than the whole eleven apostles put together. If none of them stood with Him in the hour of His need, she stood with Him. That is the kind of person the Lord wants to share His throne.

The Pouring out of the Spirit

Now I have to say that I am not like that; and I imagine many of you have to say of yourselves, "Oh, I wish to God that I could be like that, that the Spirit of the Lord could so deal with me in my routine life, so educate me, so discipline me, so train me, so bring me to the place where I give up my rights that I can express fellowship with the Lord in a moment of tremendous need and crisis.

I say I have been very nervous to bring this up because I don't think anyone will ever be able to put it more clearly, more powerfully, more beautifully than Watchman Nee when he spoke about waste. Many Christians are, by their nature, bureaucrats. They have a precision within them. They know exactly how much time to give to God and how much time not to. They can be so precise. My dear friends, devotion is always extravagant. You can never worship the Lord in a precise way, in a bureaucratic way. Real worship is the pouring out of the heart. There is within it an extravagance that nobody but the Lord Himself can understand. So here is the gospel of the kingdom.

Do you know what the Lord Jesus said about this little lady? He said, "Wheresoever this gospel is preached in the whole earth, this that she has done shall be told for a memorial or a testimony to her"; as if the Lord was saying, "I do not just want people saved, I do not even just want people spiritually educated, I want people who are in love with Me." And dear child of God, whether you are a man or whether you are a woman, that finds you, and it finds me, out. Here then is the gospel of the kingdom.

Shall we pray?

Lord, we want to thank You for that saving work that You have done in our lives in bringing us into a real experience of Your grace and of Your power; but Lord, forgive us that, so often, we hesitate when it comes to the cost. We don't know, sometimes, how to take hold of that grace of Yours to enable us to follow the whole way. We don't know, Lord, sometimes, how to take hold of that grace and that power that You have made available to us so that we can give up all right to ourselves, take up the cross and follow You. Help us, Lord, by Your Holy Spirit; minister to each one of our hearts that every one of us in this place may be enabled to say: "Lord, I will follow You. No matter what the cost, no matter what the way, I will follow You and trust You."

And, Lord, when we think of this lady and how she brought that alabaster cruse filled with that precious liquid spikenard, there are many of us that have such alabaster cruses hidden away somewhere in our lives and we have never been prepared to break it. We are almost afraid, Lord, of extravagance. We are almost afraid of too much devotion, as if, somehow, we will become fanatical or weird or unbalanced. Lord, by Your Spirit, work in all our hearts and make us people who are worshippers in spirit and in truth, those who can present their bodies a living sacrifice, holy and acceptable to Yourself as our spiritually intelligent worship.

Lord, work in us by Your Spirit. We can't do it ourselves. We commit ourselves to You. We can will to do Your will and in our hearts we can say, "I am prepared, Lord, for the cost," but only by Your Spirit can You come upon us and enable us to do what we cannot do in ourselves that is to fall into the ground and die, that is to lose our lives for Your sake and the gospel, that is to lay down our lives, our reputations, our status, our everything. Lord, You are the past master at getting camels through the eyes of needles. Do it with every one of us. Shave us of the things we trust in, Lord, and work in us in such a way that we shall have supplied to us richly that abundant entrance into the kingdom of God. We ask it in the name of our Lord Jesus. Amen.

4.
Shall Be Preached to the Whole World

Matthew 24:3–14

And as he [Jesus] sat on the mount of Olives, the disciples came unto him privately, saying, Tell us, when shall these things be? and what shall be the sign of thy coming, and of the end of the world? And Jesus answered and said unto them, Take heed that no man lead you astray. For many shall come in my name, saying, I am the Christ; and shall lead many astray. And ye shall hear of wars and rumors of wars; see that ye be not troubled: for these things must needs come to pass; but the end is not yet. For nation shall rise against nation, and kingdom against kingdom; and there shall be famines and earthquakes in divers places. But all these things are the beginning of travail. Then shall they deliver you up unto tribulation, and shall kill you: and ye shall be hated of all the nations for my name's sake. And then shall many stumble, and shall deliver up one another, and shall hate one another. And many false prophets shall arise, and shall lead many astray. And because iniquity shall be multiplied, the love of the many shall wax cold. But he that endureth to the end, the same shall be saved. And this gospel of the kingdom shall be preached in the whole world for a testimony unto all the nations; and then shall the end come.

Shall we pray:

Father, we want to thank You that we are gathered here in Your presence and that we sense already that You have been receiving us. And now, Lord, we come to Your Word and we just want to confess in Your presence that, without You, we can do nothing. I can speak, we can hear, but there will be nothing of real and eternal value out of this time unless You are our grace and power, You are our anointing. Therefore, Lord, because You have so graciously provided that anointing, we want, by faith, to appropriate it for the speaker and for the hearer alike. Dear Lord, will You, somehow, write something on our hearts and speak in such a way into our spirits that it will become flesh and blood, that it will become our very life, our very being. Lord, we commit ourselves to You now with thanksgiving in the name of our Lord Jesus. Amen.

We Have a Command

I want just to underline this one verse in Matthew's Gospel: "And this gospel of the kingdom shall be preached in the whole world for a testimony unto all the nations; and then shall the end come" (Matthew 24:14). I want to underline, first of all, this word: "This gospel of the kingdom shall be preached in the whole world." There is a command of the King that you and I should preach the gospel in the whole world. It is an imperative command. No one, no child of God, no Christian leader, no theologian has any right to contradict that command of the Lord Jesus. Almost one of the last things He said before He was taken up into the heavens was:

All authority [and power] hath been given unto me in heaven and on earth. Go ye therefore, and make disciples of all the nations, baptizing them into the name of the Father and of the Son and of the Holy Spirit: teaching them to observe all things whatsoever I commanded you: and lo, I am with you always, even unto the end of the world. Matthew 28:18b–20

In other words, we have not an if or a possibility but a commission, a command which was almost the very last thing that the Lord Jesus said to His disciples, said to those who would be His followers, said to His church, said to His redeemed. We are to go into the whole world and preach this gospel.

Mark's gospel puts it this way: "And he [Jesus] said unto them, Go ye into all the world, and preach the gospel to the whole creation" (Mark 16:15). That is an interesting word because, in a sense, it means, obviously, the inhabited earth; but it is interesting that the word is used, and so there is no getting out of this. We are not to stay in North America; we are not to stay in Europe; we are not to stay in some nice little holy huddle somewhere where things are a little more pleasant, except for the collisions we have with one another, but we are to go out into the whole world with this gospel of the kingdom.

There has been a teaching that has relegated this gospel of the kingdom to the millennium. It has made a division between the gospel of our Lord Jesus the gospel of grace and the gospel of the kingdom. It says the gospel of the kingdom is only to be preached in the millennium. I, myself, think it is so ridiculous. Anyone who has any sense at all has only to compare the words of the Lord Jesus in one gospel with the words of the Lord Jesus in another gospel and you will discover that what is called the gospel of the kingdom of God, in some, is called in others the gospel of the kingdom of heaven. Of course, we also have the gospel of the Lord Jesus and this gospel of the kingdom.

I believe this is very simple: This gospel of the kingship of God; this gospel concerning God's King; this gospel concerning the abounding grace of God by which He gives us an entrance into this kingdom and restores to us the possibility of coming to the throne of God, by the grace of God alone; this gospel of the glory of God; this gospel of our Lord Jesus; this gospel has been entrusted to those who are followers of the Lord Jesus to be preached in the whole world. We have no business to be disengaged from this commission. I want to put it in the strongest language possible. It is a sin and a transgression for the people of God not to be involved practically, relevantly in the preaching of this gospel of the kingdom in the whole world.

Now I don't know, sometimes, what is wrong with us, but we are such finite people; and I have no doubt that the Lord understands that. But for some strange reason, we are unable in our minds to contain more than one truth at a time. Once we have this truth of "gospel workers" as we call it, we will have nothing to do with conferences or with the deepening of spiritual life. We are all concentrated on evangelistic crusades, evangelistic work, missionary work, getting out to the people, and everything else. We have no time for those who, we feel, just sit at home and study their Bibles and talk about deepening of spiritual life and maturity. But likewise, those who see something of the church are often totally disengaged from gospel work, as if by seeing the purpose of God, as if by seeing the goal of God, this automatically disqualifies us and automatically, as it were, exempts us from the work of the gospel. My dear friends, there is no such thing. These two vital matters must go hand in hand. The church has to be built with living stones. But where do these living stones come from? Do we pinch them from other groups? Where do they come from? They are meant to be saved by the grace of God in our midst. They are meant, by our life and our testimony together as God's people, to come to know the Lord through our witness, through our life together, through our being conformed to the image of God's Son.

We have no business to ignore this commission of our risen and glorified King. There are those who ignore it and feel they have a right to ignore it because they are dwelling on what they feel to be more important matters that have to do with the bride, with the city of God, with the end and goal of the Lord. So they feel they are exempted. They can ignore this matter and leave it to others. Now I am not saying that all of us feel that the others are kindergarten, that they are sort of inferior; but there is a kind of atmosphere that grows just because we are normal human beings. Once we have seen something more, we feel we will leave it to those who see something less. And so we leave the whole matter of the gospel to those we feel are children. They are superficial, shallow. They don't really see this matter of the throne of God, of the bride of God, of the city of God, of the body of the Lord Jesus. So we will leave this; we can ignore this commission because we must give ourselves to a far more important matter. We cannot ignore this matter nor can we bypass it as if by concentrating on something which is essential in the purpose of God we can leave something else just as essential and just as fundamental. So we bypass it in our minds.

Then there are those who feel that once we understand something about the church as the body of the Lord Jesus and as the burden on God's heart, then this commission is virtually nullified. If we ignore or bypass or nullify this commission of the King, it is disobedience; and disobedience brings a snare and a bondage upon any life. It brings a snare and a bondage on any fellowship of God's people, any assembly of God's people.

This command is quite clear. It is to be preached in the whole world, not necessarily and only in our own homeland. It is the whole world. Now this does not mean that all of us can go to the whole world. We are not meant by this commission to become world travelers, flitting from place to place. That is not what the Lord means; but we are to have a vision that is world-wide. It is not confined to a locality or to a nation but it is a world-wide horizon. It is a world-wide vision. We are to pray for those in the front line of the battle. We are to pray for the work of the Lord in these areas of the world where it is, as it were, pioneer work. We are to pray that the Lord will help us not only to pray; sometimes, we should give; sometimes, there are many other ways in which we can be involved in this.

Then I want you to notice this: "It is until the end of the age." Our Lord gave a specific promise to those who fulfill this command: "And lo, I am with you until the end of the age." In other words, until this gospel of the kingdom has reached its goal, until it has been fulfilled in being preached in the whole world, the Lord gives us a specific promise that His presence will be with us; that is, all His grace will be with us, all His power will be with us, all His wisdom will be with us, all His resources will be available to us. The Lord has made a specific promise. I hear this promise claimed by all kinds of people who have never moved out of their homes; they have never even hardly moved out of their seat to win another person for the Lord. But this promise is conditional: We are to go and make disciples of all nations; "and lo, I am with you always, even unto the end of the age." This is not to say the Lord is not with you when you do not necessarily get involved in gospel work. But what I am saying is this: We have a specific promise that the Lord's heart is so much in this matter that He promises to be personally with us in the Person of the Holy Spirit; He promises to be with us with all His grace and all His power and all His wisdom and all His gifts and all His resources until this commission is fulfilled.

No Small Gospel

I want you to notice this is not some kind of simple gospel that is to be preached, just a gospel that proclaims that you are forgiven, that Jesus died. It is the gospel of the kingdom; that is the fullest description we have for the gospel. It includes not only the saving grace of God but the purpose of the Lord and the end of the Lord. It is very interesting what our Lord said here in Matthew: "Go ye therefore, and preach the gospel in the whole world." No. "Go ye therefore, and make converts of all nations." No. "Go ye therefore, and make members of the church." No. "Go ye therefore, and make disciples of all nations, baptizing them in the name of the Father, the Son and the Holy Ghost" (see Matthew 28:19). In other words, there you have the whole meaning of the cross; you have the whole meaning of life abundant by the Spirit of God in the meaning and testimony of baptism.

"Teaching them to observe all things that I commanded you." This is no small gospel. This is no gospel just asking for some decision, as such a hand to be put up, a little piece of paper to be signed. I do not want to devalue or despise the many who have come to know the Lord in that very simple way, but I have to tell you something. I think this term born again has been bandied about, especially in the North American media, in such a way that it has devalued the whole concept of a new birth. I fear very greatly that there are thousands upon thousands within evangelical churches, even sometimes in other fundamentalist groups, that are not truly born of God. They have entered in, in some way, with no making of their calling and election sure. I could give examples of this, but then it will take me away from what I really want to say.

God Loves Everyone in This World

We have an imperative command here, and it makes some of us feel very uncomfortable. But we have no business not to obey it. However, I want to say something else: Do you think our Lord is just interested in heads? Do you think all He wants is to get numbers into the kingdom? Do you think He wants some kind of vindication for Himself, as if that is all that He is interested in? Why did the Lord Jesus say, "And lo, I am with you always to the end of the age" unless His heart is in this matter, unless there is something so on His heart in this matter that He wants to share it with us? I know it is beyond our understanding; it is almost incredible to us; but God so loved the world that He gave His only begotten Son.

It sounds almost trite to say that God loves this world. It is very hard for me to think that the way the Lord loves me, He loves the eight hundred million Indians in the Indian subcontinent. Every one of them is loved by God and known by God. There are nearly a billion Chinese in mainland China, and every single one of them is loved by God and known by God. Now I say, that blows my mind. I think: "The Lord cannot do it. He has not got a computer big enough. He is not able, as it were, to store all the information about everyone their life, their birth, their genetic history, their temperament, their personality, the way they were born, their feelings, their longings." But there is not one in this world that is not loved by God the proud Jew, the terrorist, the British, the Germans, the Russians, the Marxists, the capitalists there is not one of them.

We can hardly take it in. There is something in us that says: "Of course, the Lord knows me; I am special. I caught His eye and the Lord said, `Well, well, look at that. There is someone there that is very special. I must take an interest in him; I will take an interest in her. She has a real personality, a flair. She has caught My eye.'" You see, we have this Islamic idea of a distant, distant God who, every now and again, impartial and impersonal as He is, looks down and His eye gets caught by a flash of color or a little explosion somewhere in this human scene and He says, "Give Me My telescope." Then He sort of fastens upon that person and studies them very carefully and says: "I think I will save that person. That is a very interesting person." This is an Islamic idea of God. It is not the God of revelation. It is not the God of Abraham, Isaac, and Jacob, the God and Father of our Lord Jesus. It is beyond us to understand that God knows every human being no matter what their color, what their race, what their background, what their condition and the Lord Jesus gave Himself for every human being.

When the Lord Jesus, in the very last moments before He ascended, said, "Go ye therefore, and make disciples of all nations," it was not that He was just saying: "I want you to do this because it is a duty, as far as I am concerned. I want heaven to be filled with trophies. I want to be able to boast about this one and that one and the other. I want all these kind of people in heaven as a sort of glory for Me." Perish the thought! The Lord Jesus loves this world. He loved it so much that He came into this world and was born in Bethlehem and lived for those thirty-three years, enduring the contradiction and gainsaying of sinners, that in the end, He might offer Himself up on the cross for the world that

He might save all those that believe, whoever they are, whatever they are. And almost the last thing He said was: "Go; go with this love that is in My heart that can be in your heart. Go and make disciples of all nations. Preach the love of God, preach the grace of God, preach the gospel that is the power of God unto salvation. Let them not only come into the kingdom of God but let them discover My heart; let them discover My purpose. Let them know that I want them to come to My throne." Oh, how we have failed in this matter.

Go to Ninevah

Then I want you to remember just one other matter in connection with this. There was a prophet, a Hebrew prophet, a Jewish prophet. He was a faithful man, a good man. He knew his Bible, he knew the covenant that God had made with our people. His name was Jonah. And one day, probably, in his quiet time God said to him, "Go to Ninevah." And Jonah said: "Ninevah! You must have made a mistake, Lord; you meant Nazareth." "No; Ninevah." "Ninevah? Never, Lord, never." And he did not wait to inquire anymore. He fled from the presence of the Lord. He went down to Joppa and bought a ticket on a boat going in the opposite direction to Ninevah. It is an amazing story. But the Lord understood His servant's heart.

This dear Jonah has become, for me, a picture of myself and has become a picture of the people of God at any given time in history. The Assyrians were the cruelest of all people. They were hateful, filled with the most abominable idolatry. Their idols were monstrous; but far more terrible than even their monstrous idols was their way of murdering other races and nations. They were the first to crucify, not by nailing to a cross but by putting a person impaled on a stake. Jonah was only interested in one thing. The Lord talked about judgment but Jonah knew the Lord a little so he felt: "I know the Lord. If I start talking about judgment and those people show the slightest sign of repentance, He will forgive them. And I am not interested in their being forgiven. I am only interested in their being liquidated." Now we may laugh, but it comes very near to us. When we have suffered, as some of us have, from other nations and other peoples, sometimes, that is exactly how we feel. We are not interested in their being saved. We are interested in the judgment of God falling on them.

Jonah got a ticket on this cargo merchant ship going in the opposite direction to Ninevah, and God arranged a storm. The storm got more and more furious, and all the sailors and the captain called upon their idols but nothing happened. Finally, someone said: "There is a man here, and he seems to know his own God. I think he might be the problem." The captain went to him and said, "Do you know anything about this storm?" And Jonah said, "Yes, it is the God of Israel." And the captain said, "What have you done?" And Jonah said, "The only way you can get rid of this storm is to throw me overboard." At least he was honest a good deal more honest than some of us. But the Lord had not only prepared a storm, He also had prepared a fish. And when Jonah was thrown overboard, he was swallowed by the fish. I believe that. I have seen enough miracles in my life to believe that God could easily produce a fish; no problem. But then we have one of the most amazing things in the whole of the Old

Testament, in fact, the whole of the Bible, really. We have a prayer meeting inside a fish's stomach.

Now there are some amazing prayer meetings at different times prayer meetings in dungeons, prayer meetings among lions, prayer meetings in fiery furnaces, all kinds of prayer meetings. But never anywhere have we ever heard of a prayer meeting inside a fish's stomach. And here is another amazing thing: Jonah remembered the word of the Lord to King Solomon: "If you will turn toward the place where I have caused My name to dwell and confess your sins, then will I hear and I will forgive and I will bring you back." How Jonah knew which way Jerusalem was, I do not know; but there in the fish's belly, he must have said, "Now, Lord, I may be facing the wrong direction, but please take it that I am facing Jerusalem"; and he prayed, "Lord, hear this prayer; I have sinned against You."

The Lord gave the poor fish a stomach ache and it coughed out Jonah on the sand. The Lord said, "Jonah, are you ready to go to Ninevah?" And Jonah said, "Yes." And you know, Jonah now said: "Well Lord, I am not going to ask anymore; I am not going to ask what You are going to do or anything. I am going to go to Ninevah and I am going to preach this gospel of judgment to Ninevah in such a way that my whole heart and being is going to be in it." And he did.

He preached, and then the most amazing thing happened. Jonah had never seen anything like this in all his years in Israel. He had preached the judgment of God, he had preached the anger of God, he had preached the covenant of God; and never had the Israelis, ever, at any point, repented. But in Ninevah, from the royal family down, the whole city the aristocracy, the nobility, the people of the city all fasted and repented; and they even put sackcloth and ashes on the cows and the horses. The Lord said: "I cannot do this thing. I am going to forgive them." Then Jonah was so upset. "Lord, You have sent me all this way; I have gone to all this trouble. I want to see these people judged. They are wicked people." "No," the Lord said.

Jonah went out in a terrible depression that many of us get when we find our theological concepts are not right. Suddenly, we discover that this whole theology we have had for years is not quite right, and we go into a deep, deep depression. He went out and he sulked. Then a gourd grew up and this awful east wind came. If you know anything about the east wind, I suspect that Jonah suffered from it. Many of us, including myself, get a certain type of headache when this ruach or this wind from the east blows strongly; and Jonah was no exception. This gourd grew up and went right over him and sheltered him. He was delighted with the greenness and the pleasantness of it.

Then a little worm got into the root and, suddenly, it died. Jonah was so upset he said: "Lord, Lord, You are perfectly capable of killing that little worm. Why did You let that worm get into this gourd?" And then the Lord said: "Jonah, you are so concerned about that gourd that came up in one day and died in a day, and you are not even the least bit bothered about this whole nation. How could I judge this nation with all these little toddlers that cannot tell their left hand from their right when their elders have repented; and what about the domestic animals?" I suggest to you that was the biggest shock Jonah ever had. The Lord knew the little toddlers in Ninevah. He actually knew all about them. It was a terrible shock to Jonah. He thought the Lord only had time for His covenant people, that He only knew the toddlers that belonged to the children of His covenant people. He knew that the Lord had said things about how to treat your donkey and how to treat your ass and your camel. It was all within the Word of God, but that was to the covenant people. He never thought that the Lord knew the domestic animals in a wicked city like Ninevah that had nothing whatsoever to do with the Promise Land. My dear friends, so often this is you and me.

When we begin to see the deeper things, when we begin to see something of the purpose of God, then somehow or other, we become exclusive, very often, and we shut out from our minds this whole world that is suffering beyond us, as if God is only interested in us and our meetings, as if we are the only recipients of His love, as if He never loved anyone else but us. He is only concerned with us; and as far as we are concerned, the sooner the Lord comes and damns the world, the better. Let it be judged, let it be destroyed, let it all go, as long as we are saved. But this gospel of the kingdom is to be preached in the whole world because God loves this world and loves it so much that He gave His only begotten Son for it, and the Lord Jesus came into this world because He loved this world. "Herein is love, not that we loved God, but that He loved us, and sent His Son to be the propitiation for our sins" (1 John 4:10). So when we begin to understand this, a whole lot of things fall into place.

The Preaching and Presence of the Kingship of God

"For a testimony unto all nations." This preaching is more than words. It is more than the definition of truth. It is more than the outlining of truth, of doctrine. It is a testimony. Now what is a testimony? A testimony has to be firsthand. It cannot be second, third, fourth-hand. You can only give a testimony, you can only be a witness if you have seen something yourself, if you were involved in some way, directly. If you were personally involved in an accident or in something that happened, then you can be a testimony, then you can give a testimony. You have to be alive to give a testimony. It has to be firsthand.

What does this mean? I think it means the preaching and the presence of the kingship of God; not just the preaching, but the presence: "Lo, I am with you all the way to the end of the age." It is not just a question of preaching, of outlining truth, of putting over theology, even though it may be sound doctrine and absolutely correct truth. The presence of the King Himself has to be there so that with the preaching of the gospel there is not only a declaration of the kingship of God but a manifestation of the kingship of God. Let me put it another way: The preaching of this gospel of the kingdom is to be authenticated by the presence of the King. So often, we have the idea that evangelism is just simply preaching some kind of message. But there should be a manifestation of the presence of the Lord, a showing forth, if you like, of the presence of the King.

I don't care how that manifestation takes place, as long as there are miracles; as long as there are lives that are torn out of the power of darkness, delivered from demonic bondage, and transferred into the kingdom of God's dear Son; as long as there are alcoholics who no longer want another drop of drink and even can come into the presence of it and have no desire for it; as long as there are broken lives made whole. These are the miracles and the signs that are the most essential thing of all. And wherever the gospel is preached, we do not expect a hundred per cent success, as if everyone who hears it is going to believe. It is to be preached for a testimony unto all nations. Our job is to declare the kingship of God; our job is to present the grace of God; and it is the work of our risen Lord, by the Spirit of God, to save those that believe.

Authentication of the Preaching of the Gospel

For those of you who have very strong views on this matter I hope you will forgive me, but I want to take it one step further. In my estimation, there is a teaching that has crippled this whole matter of the preaching of the gospel of the kingdom, and it is that we should not ever expect to see the Lord work to authenticate the preaching of the gospel. We are to preach the gospel. People are to be converts. We run it like a North American sales business with all the psychological pressure, all the salesmanship, and all the paraphernalia that goes with it. I thank God that there are signs and wonders that follow the preaching of God's Word. I personally do not believe they went out with the canon of the New Testament. I never have and never will. Maybe it is because I am Jewish, but I just cannot accept it.

When I look at church history, I find that wherever this gospel of the kingdom has been preached, whole societies have been turned upside down. For a long time, for centuries and centuries, nations have been influenced by the preaching of that gospel. The criminals got saved; the hopeless, the social outcasts got saved. Oh, I could stop and tell you story after story from the early Reformation, from the Huguenots; I could tell you stories from the early Quakers when they turned the whole of British society inside out and upside down. When two-thirds of the Quaker preachers were in prison at one time, you know what they did? So many of the inmates, the prisoners got saved that they became Bible schools; and those prisons became the Bible seminaries for Quaker preachers. When they were released, they came out by the thousands to preach the gospel. All the way through church history you find the same thing the early Methodists, the early Brethren, the early Pentecostals wherever you go you have an authentication of this preaching of the gospel of the kingdom. Mark puts it this way.

*And he said unto them, Go ye into all the world, and
preach the gospel to the whole creation ... And these signs
shall accompany them that believe: in my name shall
they cast out demons; they shall speak with new tongues;
they shall take up serpents, and if they drink any deadly
thing, it shall in no wise hurt them; they shall lay hands
on the sick, and they shall recover. Mark 16:15,17–18*

The Lord gave these marvelous examples. I know there are some groups that have snakes in their meetings and pick them up.

Can you believe it? What is the point of it? There have been cases in the Appalachian Mountains where people have drunk poison and died. But understand the point of this. What is the Lord saying? He is saying that when the gospel is preached, there is an impact of the presence of the King. It is not as if you can take poison and tempt the Lord. It is not that you see a snake and you say, "Now, I am going to pick it up in the name of the Lord." That is stupid. But the fact of the matter is this: When you are put into a situation where you can trust the Lord, He will be with you because He said, "Lo, I am with you to the end of the age." The apostle Paul said again and again: "I was not just among you in word, but in deed. My preaching was not just in wisdom but in demonstration of the Spirit and power of God." This is authentication.

"The former treatise I made, O Theophilus, concerning all that Jesus began both to do and to teach" (Acts 1:1). This is Luke who by the Spirit of God wrote Acts. He had also written the Gospel of Luke. Now he tells us a most amazing thing. Jesus is at the right hand of the majesty on high, and here are 120 members of His body filled with the resurrection life and power of the Lord Jesus through the Person of the Holy Spirit; and suddenly, the whole thing begins again. All that Jesus had done, the early church does. There are miracles, there are signs, there are marvelous things happening. Now don't get me wrong. There are Jameses that get beheaded and Peters that have angels come to them and unlock every gate and take them out. You will never understand the sovereignty of the Lord in this matter. But the fact of the matter is this: As we read through the book of Acts, we discover that the body is the actual body of the Lord Jesus. The Head is still working through His body on earth, turning the world upside down, confronting them with the kingship of God, confronting them with the kingdom of God, confronting them with the power of God, confronting them with the truth of God. This is this gospel.

Where has this idea come from that gospel preaching is an evangelistic meeting where we simply preach a simple gospel? Now please, don't get me wrong on this thing. I thank God for the gospel, wherever it is preached. I thank God for the way the Lord uses people. I think of Charles Haddon Spurgeon. When he was a boy, he went into a little chapel in a village somewhere in Essex in east England and heard a man who could hardly speak the Queen's English. He preached the simplest gospel, and Spurgeon said, "I could count every mistake he made." Then the power of God fell on Spurgeon, and the great Charles Haddon Spurgeon was saved. I would not despise some dear brother preaching simply out of his heart by the power of God; but where has this idea come that gospel work is somehow confined to an evangelistic meeting? Where does it come from? Surely, we need to get out.

Preaching of the Gospel Operative to the End

There is another phrase in this verse I just want to underline: "Then shall the end come." "And this gospel of the kingdom shall be preached in the whole world for a testimony unto all the nations; and then shall the end come." In other words, the preaching of the gospel of the kingdom for a testimony to all nations is operative to the very end. We have no business to say that we will not be able to do it, that we should not bother about it because now we are in the very last days. Right through to the end, this gospel of the kingdom is to be preached. It is to be fulfilled in the midst of enormous upheaval and turmoil, in the midst of much persecution and tribulation and affliction, and antagonism from the society around us. This gospel of the kingdom has to be preached as a testimony unto all nations.

Signs of the Time

Where are we in this age? Of course, if we look at Matthew 24, we have a whole lot of signs that our Lord gave us about kingdom rising against kingdom and nation against nation, about famines and earthquakes and plague diseases and persecution. This last century has seen two world wars and a whole generation or two that has lived in nothing but the rumor of war. It has only been, literally, in the last year that the thing has begun to relax a little. And that is only another stage in the fulfillment of God's prophetic Word. The fact of the matter is we have never seen wars like we have seen in this century. We have never seen such turmoil; we have never seen such upheaval. With it, there have been earthquakes and more to come. There have been famines and many more to come and the reason being that, ecologically, we have damaged the earth, probably, beyond redemption until the Lord Jesus returns to put it right. We are seeing the beginning of such things as plague diseases. And persecution has there been any century in the whole history of the church and of Israel when more people have become martyrs for the name of our Lord Jesus than in this last century?

In the midst of it, the fig tree is suddenly found back in its own soil; the judged fig tree, the withered fig tree, the fig tree that disappeared altogether from its soil is suddenly back in its soil and very lively. They have tried to kill that fig tree again and again and again in the last forty years and have done nothing but make it more virile and more powerful. We think of the words of the Lord Jesus: "And Jerusalem shall be trodden down of the Gentiles, until the times of the Gentiles be fulfilled" (Luke 21:24). Now I am not going into politics on this, I am just saying these are the words of the Lord Jesus. Whatever we think about the politics, whatever we feel about the Middle East situation, the fact of the matter is, you have a Jewish nation there for the first time in 2000 years. That fig tree is back in its soil, and that Jerusalem is no longer trodden down by non-Jews. These are the words of the Lord Jesus.

Where are we in this age? We must be near to the coming of the kingdom. We have to be; and if we look now at our present situation, suddenly we discover, to our amazement, that something happens in the Marxist world which is altogether unbelievable. It happens in Poland; it goes from Poland to Hungary, from Hungary to Bulgaria, from Bulgaria to East Germany, from East Germany to Czechoslovakia, from Czechoslovakia to Romania. It is unbelievable; and suddenly, a whole area of the world that has been in the most iron-like bondage is released. They are having open airs in Warsaw, open airs in Budapest. Believers are being allowed to meet together freely. They can have Bible studies and prayer meetings, circulate letters and print Bibles. It is the most unbelievable thing that has happened. A man who knows the Lord has come to the presidency of the Czechoslovak people. Another man at least a committed, observant Catholic has become prime minister of another one of those countries. It is unbelievable.

How is it that a person like I didn't even know it heretofore? I didn't know it when I was here last year. Wouldn't it have been lovely if I could have said to you: "Now watch. In a few months, this is going to happen." You would have said, "Rubbish!" After it happened, I would not even have had to say to you, "There you are." I would have kept quiet, and you would have come to me and said: "You said that last year. That was remarkable." But I was as blind as anybody else in this matter.

Think of the Kremlin. Who would have ever thought that the Kremlin would allow a Christian service to be televised to the whole of the Soviet Union on Orthodox Christmas eve? It is unbelievable. I am not saying that the whole thing is wonderful. Of course not; there are still Marxists in charge of the Kremlin. But something unbelievable is happening. We are on the threshold of a one-world leadership and a one-world government because the whole West has now got to do something about shoring up these nations, and even the Soviet Union, less they revert to a far worse totalitarianism. And so we are very near to a one world. We don't want it. Many of the nations of the West, including the United States, don't want it; but I believe there will be a voluntary surrender of sovereignty on the part of many, many nations in the interest of world peace and world prosperity. We are so near to it.

I think of Germany; I think of the European Common Market. It has come about in the most unbelievable way. When I was first saved, this old Swedish aunt said to me, "The Holy Roman Empire will be revived." Now I was interested in this because I had some relatives who were connected with the aristocratic families of Hapsburg. "Oh yes," she said. "It is going to go right across here and right across there; it is going to take in this and take in this." This was in l944.

It is amazing what is happening in Europe, especially if Hungary comes into this and Czechoslovakia, as it must, and Eastern Germany and, probably, part of Yugoslavia, possibly even part of Poland, if not the whole of Poland. Then we have a most amazing thing. We have the growth of a block of nations in Europe that is destined to be the most powerful, the most wealthy, and the most influential factor in world history for the last part of the age.

In the beginning of the 30's, there were two nations in this world that were governed by a demonic, pagan principality. One was Germany, and the other was Japan. Both of them endlessly spoke of a new world order. They talked and talked until they were blue in the face about this new world order that they were going to bring to the world. The Nazis were going to the whole of Europe in a great Reich that was going to last a thousand years and was going to stretch from the Atlantic to the Urals. The whole of Asia, China mainland, Manchuria, and all southeast Asia were going to come into this great empire of Japan under the sun god. They tried to do it by military means and they failed; and it is interesting that these two nations have become the great economic miracles of the post Second World War period.

With the decline of America which I think is almost irreversible suddenly, we discover Germany is going to reunite, not over years but almost within weeks, by July 1 with a common currency, and a common administration. There is no doubt at all that Germany will be the greatest and most influential single factor in the European Common Market. And isn't it interesting that when Eastern Europe called upon the United States to help and she felt she was unable to fully help, as she wanted to, the United States called upon Germany to do something? Germany said, "We cannot do anything because we are going to try and shore up East Germany." So Germany called on Japan; and the prime minister of Japan came straight to Bonn. He gave an unbelievable speech, which I think will mark, in days to come in history, one of the new turning points of world history. He said, "We are on the brink of a new world order."

My dear friends, don't be afraid. This is most exciting. This means that you and I are just where Revelation 13 is. You and I are actually here in Matthew 24. Now here is the positive thing. We have a commission to preach the gospel of the kingdom in the whole world as a testimony unto all nations. We don't know how long we have, but I have no doubt there is a harvest to be reaped, and you and I need to be involved in it.

The Challenge

Out of this comes an unavoidable challenge, and it is this: How much are you, how much am I involved in this gospel of the kingdom being preached in the whole world? My dear friends, as one gets older, you reflect more. If I had my time all over again, I would put a much greater emphasis on supporting those dear servants of God in the far-flung parts of this world. It has been my privilege to travel in many places in the tropical rain forest, in the deserts and I have sometimes had to go alone to my room because I thought, from my background, I should not cry in public. Sometimes, I have been so moved. I could keep you here for an hour talking about different ones by name, the faithful, servants of the Lord who have given their lives for tribes, suffered unbelievably, lived on a shoestring, who have hardly been known here in the West not hardly prayed for, let alone supported. If I had my time over again, with the little understanding I have of the church, the little I have of the purpose of God, the little I have of the absolute necessity of being built together and related together, I would put myself unreservedly behind these people.

I remember on one occasion when an old lady approached me. She was dressed in a certain way, had a certain look about her; and because she was not used to the West or the ways of the West, she stood away from me and bowed her head. I said to her, "Do you want to say something?" "Yes," she said. And I said: "Where are you from? Are you from Indonesia?" "Indonesia," she said. "No; I am not from Indonesia; I am from Naka Land." "Naka Land." I said. "Do you know where Naka is?" I said, "I do"; and I told her exactly where it was and a big smile came across her face. Then she said to me: "Dear brother, I want to tell you that we pray for you in all our assemblies. Eighty-five per cent of the Naka people have come to know the Lord Jesus, and we pray for you everywhere. If you could only come to us sometime." I thank God for whoever it was who first took the gospel to those people.

On another occasion, a person approached me in yet another place, in Thailand, and I didn't know who they were. They were obviously from one of the tribes, and I said, "Where do you come from?" "I come from the Burmese border," he said. "What are you?" And he said, "Liuzhou. You have no idea how we love Israel, how we pray for Israel. We believe the purpose of God for us as the body of the Lord Jesus, somehow, is related to what God is doing in that nation." I remembered Dr. Frazier of Liuzhou Land. I remembered the great prayer battle and how he agonized in prayer for those Liuzhou people until, finally, God saved the first family. It is amazing what has happened to the Liuzhou people. Three quarters of them have come to know the Lord Jesus.

Oh, the challenge! Then I think to myself: "Where have I been? What have I been doing?" When I was first saved, I believed that the Lord was calling me to China, and therefore, my studies were in that light. I was accepted by a certain mission and put on their books. I remember that in my studies at the university, I had to study about Mongolia and then Tibet and then Korea and then the Manchu people; and I became more and more burdened. I was young. I remember, one day, I went to my room and I said to the Lord, "Lord, I wish I had ten lives because I would give one to Tibet and one to Mongolia and one to the Manchu people and one to Korea and one to this." Then my health failed, and China went Communist; and I could not understand. Why did the Lord call me? Why did He put this burden in my heart?

Some years ago when I was going to bed by then I was deeply involved in the work in Britain I heard a voice behind me say, "Return to your own people." And I thought to myself, "Who are my own people?" I knew they were not the English. I thought to myself, "Who?" Then I went to bed. How gracious the Lord was. He did not bother me for three and a half months. Then I was going to bed again and exactly the same thing happened. The voice behind me said, "Return to your own people." And this time I thought: "I know this is the Lord, but how can I tear myself away from this work that I have been an integral part of for all these years? I just can't walk out on them. I don't know how it will happen." How gracious the Lord is. He never bothered me. He left me for another few months. The same thing happened again as I was going to bed, and I heard this voice behind me: "Return to your own people." Now this time, I said: "Yes, I know Lord. I know who You mean. I have known it from the beginning." But I didn't want to face it. Then I said: "Lord, don't be angry with me. I am old enough now not to need signs and confirmations. I know You speak to me; but Lord, You know nobody is going to understand this; and because I am a person who is thorough, I will go through agonies. Lord, don't be angry. You give me a home in Jerusalem, and I will know that You are in this." Well, I can only tell you the Lord fell over Himself doing that; the most unbelievable things happened.

Then I went back to my own people; and miraculously, I was given citizenship and then given a quite honored place with much contact with many people in very powerful positions. Suddenly, instead of being trapped in the British Isles in Europe, I began to travel. Then I began to find things. When I have been in Borneo, when I have been in Thailand, when I have been in Indonesia, when I have been in many of these places and seen what God is doing, my heart has become more and more burdened. Oh, how I wish with all my heart that God would disturb us so that we would have a heart for the world. When I first saw those people in the Philippines in the garbage dumps, I cried. I never thought there could be people who lived in such circumstances made in the image of God, loved by God, and nobody caring. The Filipinos have become maids and servants all over the world, prostitutes, and nobody cares.

My dear friends, don't hide in the truth of God's eternal purpose. Don't hide in the truth concerning the body of our Lord Jesus. These are on the heart of God; but remember, we have a commission. We just can't go out of duty. It is the love of God that has to be shed abroad in our hearts that will bring us to a place where, perhaps, we shall come into an involvement with this preaching of the gospel of the kingdom in the whole world for a testimony. From every tribe, from every tongue, from every kindred, from every nation treasure for the city of God. May the Lord put this on your heart. May you never again be able to relegate the gospel to the kindergarten. May the Lord burn it into your spirit, as I pray He burns it into mine, and give us a heart that is like His.

Shall we pray?

Lord, we lift up our hearts to You. Forgive us that so often, we don't have any time at all for that work in the nations. Lord, will You do something in our hearts? And will You bring us face to face with this commission of Yours to preach the gospel in the whole creation. Help us, Lord; help us to start where You would have us start with our hearts. Open up these hearts of ours in the way that You changed Jonah so that he could tell the story against himself. Deal with our hearts that we may have a heart of love and a heart of compassion, a heart whose horizon is the whole world. Lord, give us that passion that You have; give us into our spirits, that travail that You have, that out of every tongue and kindred and people and nation there shall come treasure for Your city. You are calling out a people, Lord. Will You help us to be practically and relevantly involved? And we ask it in the name of our Lord Jesus. Amen.

Other books by Lance Lambert

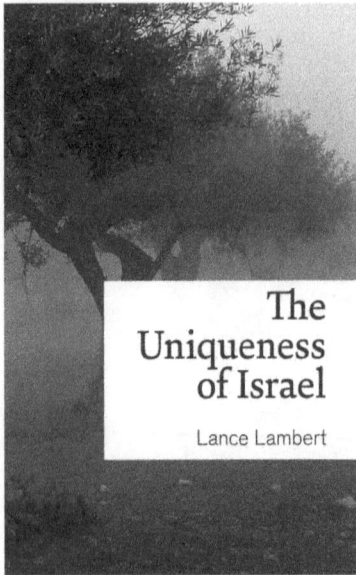

The Uniqueness of Israel

Woven into the fabric of Jewish existence there is an undeniable uniqueness. There is bitter controversy over the subject of Israel, but time itself will establish the truth about this nation's place in God's plan. For Lance Lambert, the Lord Jesus is the key that unlocks Jewish history He is the key not only to their fall, but also to their restoration. For in spite of the fact that they rejected Him, He has not rejected them.

Till The Day Dawns

Lance Lambert

Till the Day Dawns

"And we have the word of prophecy made more sure; whereunto ye do well that ye take heed, as unto a lamp shining in a dark place, until the day dawn, and the day-star arise in your hearts." (II Peter 1:9).

The word of prophecy was not given that we might merely be comforted but that we would be prepared and made ready. Let us look into the Word of God together, searching out the prophecies, that the Day-Star arise in our hearts until the Day dawns.

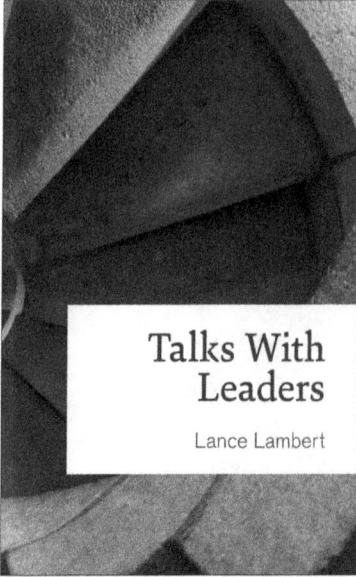

Talks With
Leaders

Lance Lambert

Talks With Leaders

"O Timothy, guard that which is committed unto thee ..." (I Timothy 6:20) Has God given you something? Has God deposited something in you? Is there something of Himself which He has given to you to contribute to the people of God? Guard it. Guard that vision which He has given you. Guard that understanding that He has so mercifully granted to you. Guard that experience which He has given that it does not evaporate or drain away or become a cause of pride. Guard that which the Lord has given to you by the Holy Spirit. In these heart-to-heart talks with leaders Lance Lambert covers such topics as the character of God's servants, the way to serve, the importance of anointing, and hearing God's voice. Let us consider together how to remain faithful with what has been entrusted to us.

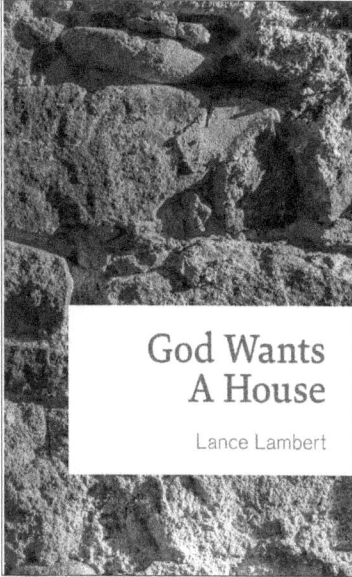

God Wants a House

Where is God at home? Is He at home in Richmond, VA? Is He at home in Washington? Is He at home in Richmond, Surrey? Is He at home in these other places? Where is God at home? There are thousands of living stones, many, many dear believers with real experience of the Lord, but where has the ark come home? Where are the staves being lengthened that God has finally come home? In God Wants a House Lance looks into this desire of the Lord, this desire He has to dwell with His people. What would this dwelling look like? Let's seek the Lord, that we can say with David, "One thing have I asked of Jehovah, that will I seek after: that I may dwell in the house of Jehovah all the days of my life, To behold the beauty of Jehovah, And to inquire in his temple."